Through Our Own Eyes

A Journey Into African American History

A Curriculum Guide for Parents and Teachers

By: Joseph Edelin, M.Ed.

Published in partnership with Project Ujima, LLC

Decatur, GA

www.project-ujima.com

©2019

ISBN: 978-1-70-480526-9

Project Ujima, LLC is an educational consulting company that provides culturally relevant and responsive content to districts, schools, and teachers, in the form of workshops and resources, that are geared toward raising student achievement.

Dedication

To the Ancestors, this book is BECAUSE of you. To the next generation, this book is FOR you. To my friends and family, this book couldn't have been completed without your love and support. Lastly, to my father, I felt your presence guiding me every day while I was writing this book, I hope you are proud of what we have accomplished.

Table of Contents

Introduction

There is an African proverb that states, "Until the lions have their own historians, the story of the hunt will continue to glorify the hunter." That quote in its essence is the reason why I became an educator and is the entire purpose behind this book.

As a student, I remember learning extensively about the myths and legends of Ancient Greece and Rome, the feats of Alexander the Great, the accomplishments of the Enlightenment thinkers, and the bravery of our "founding fathers" as they fought the American Revolution. Throughout it all, I remember thinking to myself, "What does this have to do with me? Where are all the black people?" For the majority of my elementary and secondary education the only time I was able to experience black people in school was when they were picking cotton, being whipped, or were one of the three recurring Civil Rights activists discussed during the shortest month of the year. I figured that's all there was.

It was not until my matriculation through Morehouse College that I realized a great injustice had been done to me by my teachers and my school district. It was at Morehouse that I learned and realized the extent to which, as Lerone Bennett Jr. put it, "The history taught in our schools is a false history, a history of lies, omissions and distortions."

My experience was not an isolated one. Throughout this country, the stories of people of color have not been and currently still are not being told. In its stead a one-sided, white-washed tale has been inserted. This carefully redacted story puts on a pedestal those who are responsible for the enslavement, death, rape, degradation, subordination, and discrimination of hundreds of millions of people throughout the history of the world. Simultaneously, this same story relegates all people of color, but specifically people of African descent, to the status of cultural and historical phenomena, having materialized in this world with no background, no accomplishments and no civilization of any kind.

Well, what effect does this rendering have on those who hear it? For one group, it instills in them a sense of pride and accomplishment. It shows them what they can do and what's possible because they have seen examples of it. For the other group, it creates a sense of shame; their sense of self depreciates, their appreciation and respect for their own racial group turns contemptuous. They develop what Chike Akua calls "cultural amnesia". They do not know who they are, where they came from, or how they got here. Well, when you don't know who you are, then you are forced to become someone else, take on a foreign identity, a foreign culture, and admire a foreign history since you don't know your own.

Through Our Own Eyes was created for those teachers, parents and students who want to correct the biased narrative that occurs in most American schools and classrooms. It is my goal to try and fill in the often-missing pages of history by telling the story of African American people from its earliest beginnings, all the way through the Civil Rights Movement; while providing relevant and rigorous educational activities and resources that help students stay engaged and retain the information. Within this book, I have written text about some of the most important people, civilizations, events and groups throughout African and African American history, however the list is in no way exhaustive. Black history is so gloriously expansive that I could not have hoped to have covered all of it in this limited space. Despite that, I hope that as you read, answer the questions, complete the activities, and watch the videos, that it ignites a desire to explore deeper, and uncover as much as you can about the richness of African American history. Enjoy!

How You Should Use This Book

I wrote *Through Our Own Eyes* so that it can be used by parents and teachers to supplement the curriculum their children are receiving in school. My hope is that it will help fill in the gaps where the contributions and accomplishments of black people should have been, and students will be able to get a clear and complete view of the role that people of African descent have played in the forming of our global civilization.

This book contains a variety of original texts that flow in chronological order, illuminating African American history from the earliest points in human society on the continent of Africa, all the way through the Civil Rights Movement in the United States. When engaging with the texts, it is best to read them in order, from earliest to latest, so that students can understand the complete flow of historical events. However, if you want to focus on a particular time period in history, the book is also broken down into sections that group civilizations, people, and events according to their historical epoch.

The texts themselves are meant for late elementary school, middle school, and high school students. While the texts are meant for students to read on their own, to help develop their reading comprehension skills, teachers should work with their students as they read to ensure that they are fully grasping the information. I also encourage parents to engage in the reading and activities with their children, so as to make learning an activity that the whole family can do together. To accompany each text, I have included five reading comprehension questions that assesses what students have read so that you, as a parent or teacher, can determine if they understood what the content.

According to research conducted by American educator Edgar Dale, in the long term, students only retain 10% of the information that they read, however that when they actually do some sort of hands on activity with that same information, they can retain up to 80% of it in their long-term memory. It is for that reason that I have included three activities to go along with each text that requires students to delve deeper into the content. On some occasions the activities require the students to do additional research on the topic; in other areas it might ask the students to create something related to that text. Regardless of the type of activity, they are all meant to stretch the students' thinking and create a connection between them and the content; which will help them internalize the information they are learning.

One of the biggest cries for help that I hear from math and science teachers is how they would love to incorporate more culturally relevant activities into their classroom, but that it is hard to do so because so much of it has to do with content usually found in a history class. I completely understand their frustration, so I wanted to make sure I included a section called *Cross Curricular Connections* that linked each text to math and science concepts, hopefully making it easier for teachers of those subjects to include the information in their classes. The questions in the *Cross Curricular Connections* are meant to improve the students' skills in math by having them apply certain mathematical concepts to different historical situations. Similarly, students will be shown how the content in the text relates to a certain scientific concept or idea, and they must research that concept to learn more about it. Hopefully by using the *Cross Curricular Connections* section, teachers will be able to add more tools to their "teacher tool belt", and students will be able to see how the accomplishments of African American people span far beyond that depicted by most history textbooks.

Finally, to accommodate the more visual learners, embedded within each text, I have included QR codes that link to various YouTube videos that are related to each text. This is just another avenue that parents, teachers, and students can use to access the information about each subject.

Ancient African History
[65 Million BCE - 1591 ACE]

"African history is simply the missing pages of world history."
- Arturo Alfonso Schomburg

The Beginning of the Human Race

There are many theories about how human life started on earth. Scientists who believe in the theory of evolution believe that human beings evolved from primates over a period of millions of years. Experts believe the first "human" appeared 3.2 million years ago in Africa. This first human ancestor was known as a hominid, because it was a primate that walked upright on two legs. Specifically, it was called Australopithecus, which meant "southern dwelling ape". The first human ancestor resembled a hybrid between a monkey and a very small human. It would have been about 3 feet tall, possibly covered in fur, and walked on two legs.

The first human ancestor is believed to have lived in the region of Africa that is currently known as Tanzania. Specifically, she lived in an area called the Olduvai Gorge which is near Lake Victoria,

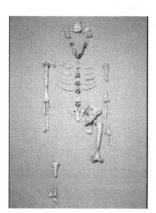

Africa's largest lake. An archeologist named Donald Johanson, along with a team of Ethiopian archeologists, found the oldest known skeleton that has the most similarities to a human skeleton in the Olduvai Gorge. The scientists named the skeleton "Lucy" because when they found her, the song that was playing on the radio was "Lucy in the Sky with Diamonds" by The Beatles. However, the Africans with Johanson called her Dinqnesh in their own African language, which means "wonderful". Scientists have found many other fossilized skeletons in Africa, but through *carbon dating,* the process of measuring the amount of the element of carbon in a once living being to determine how old it is, they have found that

Dinqnesh's skeleton is the oldest and therefore they call her the oldest human relative.

The location of the Olduvai Gorge is a very important detail when discussing what early human beings looked like. The Olduvai Gorge is about 100 miles south of the equator in East Africa. This means that the temperature in the area was very hot and that the sun was very strong. People who are from places where the sun is intense produce a chemical in their skin called melanin. Melanin is a chemical produced by the body that gives the body it's color. It also protects against the sun's ultraviolet rays, which can cause skin cancer. People who come from places with a strong sun have darker skin because their body produces more melanin to protect themselves against the sun. If Lucy was the first person on earth and she was found in an area of Africa with a strong, hot sun, then Lucy probably had very dark skin. This means that the first person on earth was probably a black person!

Many people throughout history have tried to say that black people do not have a history before slavery and that they have not contributed to the progress and accomplishments of the human race, outside of the areas of sports and entertainment. The existence of Dinqnesh proves that the original people on earth came from Africa and that if it were not for African people, the human race would not exist.

Show What You Know! – The Beginning of the Human Race

Reading For Understanding
1. Write a complete sentence that describes what the first human looked like using at least three adjectives.

   _____

   _____

   _____

2. The earliest human ancestor was given two names. What were they and why was she given those names?

   _____

   _____

   _____

3. What is melanin? Describe two things that melanin does for human beings.

   _____

   _____

   _____

4. Explain how you could prove that the first person on earth was a black person.

   _____

   _____

   _____

5. Why is it important to know that the first person on earth was from Africa and was a black person?

   _____

   _____

   _____

Take it to the Next Level
1. Research the following prompt: If the first human beings came from Africa and had melanin, then where did all of the other races of the world come from? Present your findings in a five-paragraph essay or through a PowerPoint presentation.
2. Based on the text, draw what you think Dinqnesh and her surrounding environment looked like when she was living.
3. The first human was given two names: Lucy and Dinqnesh. By which name do you think she should be called and why?

Cross-curricular Connections
Math: If Lucy/Dinqnesh's fossilized bones prove that she lived 3.2 million years ago, and the first modern humans began migrating out of Africa about 250,000 years ago, for how many years did the first humans stay in Africa?
Science: Research and create a presentation on the different functions and benefits that melanin has on the body.

The Ancient Kingdom of Nubia

The Ancient Kingdom of Nubia, sometimes referred to the Kingdom of Kush, was one of the first African civilizations that ever existed. The Kingdom of Nubia could be found south of Egypt in the current country of Sudan. Some of its major cities were Qustal, Meroe, and Khartoum. It lasted from around 3800 B.C.E. to 652 A.C.E. The word Nubia came from an Ancient Egyptian word *nub* that means "gold", so Nubia meant

"The Land of Gold". It was called this because of the great gold mines that could be found there that supplied Egypt with its gold. The Nubians were the people who lived in Nubia; however, they called their land Ta-Seti which meant, "Land of the Bow" this referred to the amazing archers the Nubians had in their armies.

Nubia supported Egypt by providing its supplies such as food, gold, spices, ivory, and animal skins. Nubia also gave Egypt its system of government, religion, and many of its traditions and celebrations. Basically, Nubia was where Egypt's culture developed. It was also one of the first completely black civilizations ever. Besides providing Ancient Egypt with its supplies and culture, Nubia was also known for its many pyramids that were built in honor of its kings and queens.

There was a total of 223 pyramids built in Nubia, while the Egyptians only built around 100 pyramids. Many people assume that the Nubian pyramids were tombs and that the kings and queens of Nubia were buried inside of them, however that was not always the case. The pyramids were built as a monument to the rulers as a symbol of the love and respect the citizens had for them.

Nubia still holds many clues to how the greatest civilizations started in Africa, and it needs to be studied to learn more. Unfortunately, this is almost impossible because nearly all of the ancient land of Nubia is under the water of a man-made lake called Lake Nasser. Lake Nasser was created after the Aswan High Dam was built on the Nile River to produce hydroelectric power for Egypt in 1960 ACE. As water began to collect behind the dam, it created Lake Nasser (named after an Egyptian president). Forty Nubian villages had to be moved, 18 temples and monuments had to be relocated (6 were moved to Europe), and thousands of people were moved off of their land. Additionally, an unknown number of people were drowned because they refused to be forced off of their ancient land. The creation of Lake Nasser essentially submerged centuries of African artifacts and accomplishments, never to be seen again.

One of the temples that had to be moved was Abu Simbel. The temple of Abu Simbel was carved out of a mountain by hand beginning in the year 1244 BCE and took 20 years to complete. The temple was built for the Egyptian pharaoh (king) Ramses II and was called by the people at that time The Temple of Ramses. It was dedicated to Ramses and several important Ancient Egyptian gods, and twice a year, on October 20th, Ramses' birthday, and February 20th, the anniversary of when Ramses became pharaoh; a beam of

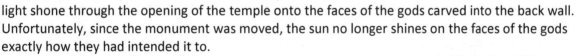

light shone through the opening of the temple onto the faces of the gods carved into the back wall. Unfortunately, since the monument was moved, the sun no longer shines on the faces of the gods exactly how they had intended it to.

As one of the greatest, and most influential of the ancient African civilizations, the Kingdom of Nubia has left its permanent mark on the world. However, there is still so much that has yet to be discovered about this amazing civilization that its true impact is still unknown.

Show What You Know! – The Ancient Kingdom of Nubia

Reading for Understanding

1. What does the word Nubia mean? Why was it called that?

_____

_____

_____

2. What does Ta-Seti mean? Why was that a name used by the Nubians to describe their country?

_____

_____

_____

3. Describe three ways that Nubia had an impact on Ancient Egypt.

_____

_____

_____

4. Why is it difficult for people today to study the history of the Kingdom of Nubia?

_____

_____

_____

5. Describe four facts about the temple of Abu Simbel.

_____

_____

_____

Take it to the Next Level

1. An acrostic poem is a poem that uses each of the letters in a specific word to create sentences that describes that word. Each letter in the word must be used to begin each sentence. Create an acrostic poem from the word NUBIA.
2. Imagine you were a descendant from the ancient Nubians and you are watching as Lake Nasser begins to cover the land and buildings that your ancestors built thousands of years ago. Write a journal entry describing your reaction to this event.
3. Research the temple of Abu Simbel and based on your research build your own model of the temple.

Cross-curricular Connections

Math: If the Ancient Nubian civilization started in 3800 BCE and ended in 652 ACE, how many years did the civilization last?

Science: The Aswan High Dam, which created Lake Nasser was built to help generate electricity for Egypt by using hydroelectric power. Research the benefits and drawbacks of hydroelectric power. In addition, research another form of alternative energy that could have been used to generate electricity for Egypt.

10

Ancient Egypt/Kemet

Ancient Egypt is arguably one of the most fascinating civilizations of all time. Images of towering pyramids, masks made of gold, and mummies rising out of their tombs are often depicted in films, documentaries, and books throughout the globe. Unfortunately, Ancient Egypt is not always portrayed correctly due to a lack of factual information that has been passed on through textbooks and other forms of media over the last several decades. In order to correctly understand the impact that African people have had on world history, Ancient Egypt must be properly studied and the true details must be uncovered about this magnificent ancient civilization.

Egypt is located in the northeastern corner of Africa. Most of the land in Egypt is covered by the hot and dry Sahara Desert. The Nile River, Egypt's main fresh water source, flows directly through Egypt.

The Nile River (called the Hapi River by the Africans) was very important to the Ancient Egyptians. Every year, the Nile River would inundate, or flood, onto the land. After the water levels returned to normal, the flood would leave very fertile soil called silt on the ground. The silt made it possible for plants to grow and for farmers to plant crops. This allowed the people of Ancient Egypt to settle in that area and build up their civilization instead of having to chase and follow food like so many other ancient groups had to do.

The original people in Egypt were black Africans. They were proud of their black skin and even named their country Kemet which means "The Land of the Black People." The name Egypt was a name that was given to Kemet by the Ancient Greeks when they invaded and conquered it. It comes from the Greek word Aegyptos, which means "land of the burnt faces". The images you see in movies and on television shows of Ancient Egyptians who have light or tan skin is not true. In real life, they were a dark-skinned people, with African features like full lips, wide noses and curly hair, sometimes worn in locks or braids. Today, the people in Egypt are lighter-skinned because they have mixed with many white and tan skinned races over hundreds of years.

The black people of Kemet were part of an advanced civilization that created the foundation on which many other civilizations were built. The Kemetic people were the first to ever develop a system of writing. They called it Medu Neter, which meant "Divine Speech," but the Greeks renamed it hieroglyphics. These ancient Africans were also the first people to ever make paper. They called it papyrus, which is where our modern-day word for paper comes from. They even built some of the most amazing buildings and sculptures like the pyramids, and the Sphinx. They had a very advanced system of science and mathematics which allowed them to understand how the planets and stars moved, thus enabling them to develop a calendar system that is even more accurate than the one we use today!

The mysteries and wonders of Kemet continue to shock and amaze both young and old alike, however people need to realize that Kemet had a lot more to offer the world than just pyramids, and mummies. This ancient black civilization that started in Africa had an immeasurable impact and influence on not just African history, but also on the history of the world.

Show What You Know! – Ancient Egypt/Kemet

Reading for Understanding

1. Why was the Nile River important to the Ancient Egyptians? What impact did the Nile River have on the development of Ancient Egyptian history and civilization?

   _____

   _____

   _____

2. What did the word Kemet mean? Why was it called that? Where does the word Egypt come from?

   _____

   _____

   _____

3. Why do people living in Egypt today have lighter skin than the people who originally inhabited the country?

   _____

   _____

   _____

4. Why are many of the words used to describe Ancient Egypt words from Greece and not African words?

   _____

   _____

   _____

5. List three inventions that the Ancient Egyptian/Kemetic people created.

   _____

   _____

   _____

Take it to the Next Level

1. Create a poem, or rap about what you just learned from the text about Ancient Egypt/Kemet.
2. Write a paragraph explaining your opinion on the following prompt: Is it important to know that the original people of Ancient Egypt/Kemet were black? Why or why not?
3. Research the different letters in the Metu Neter/hieroglyphics and write your full name. In your opinion, would it be easier or harder to write in Medu Neter than in your current language? Explain your answer.

Cross Curricular Connection

Math: The first dynasty in Kemet is believed to have started around 3400 BCE. How many years ago did that first dynasty begin?

Science: One of the aspects of Ancient Kemet that was made famous by movies and television shows was the idea of mummies. Interestingly, mummification was a real process that Kemetic people used to preserve the bodies of people who died. Research the mummification process, and describe using words or pictures, a step by step process of how it was done.

Kemetic Architectural Achievements

The people of Kemet developed some of the world's first architecture. It was very advanced and was based on their in depth understanding of math and science. Many of their structures, including the Pyramids of Giza, the Great Sphinx, as well as hundreds of temples and monuments are still standing today, even after thousands of years.

Pyramids were large stone structures that were built in honor of the pharaoh (king or queen), and a place where his body was placed after he/she died. It was also believed that the pyramids helped guide his/her soul to the Underworld, the place the Kemetic people believed everybody went to when they died. They were the world's first skyscrapers and were extremely difficult to build. Some of the pyramids were over 400 feet tall, which is almost twice as tall as the Statue of Liberty! Scientists today still have a hard time explaining how the Kemetic people designed and built pyramids with their lack of electronic and gas-powered technology.

The Step Pyramid was the first pyramid ever built, it was designed for the pharaoh Djoser (pronounced Zoser) by the world's first multi-genius, Imhotep. The Great Pyramid, was built for the Pharaoh Khufu, it is the largest pyramid in the world and can be found at the city of Giza in Egypt. It is

surrounded by several other pyramids that were built for other pharaohs. The Great Pyramid, took around 20 years to build with more than 15,000 people working on it almost around the clock. Most pyramids were constructed out of a yellowish type of rock called limestone, that could be found in many places around Kemet called quarries. The limestone would be cut by hand into large stone blocks that weighed about 4000 pounds each and loaded onto boats or logs and transported to the site where the pyramid was to be built. In order to add levels onto the pyramid, large ramps had to be built so that the heavy blocks could be pushed and pulled up to the next level. Once all of the levels had been constructed, a large triangular piece was placed at the top, which was usually made out of gold or silver. The final step was to smooth out the sides with white limestone and place the pharaoh inside the pyramid as his final resting place. The pyramids could be seen from many miles away, shining like white diamonds in the desert sun.

There is an image that often accompanies the building of the pyramids of slaves being whipped as they pulled and pushed the heavy blocks that were needed to build the pyramids. This image is false, as the people who built the pyramids were skilled, paid workers. Many of the people who built the pyramids volunteered to work on these projects because they wanted to honor the pharaoh, who many people believed was the representation of God on earth.

Another well-known structure from Kemet was the Sphinx. The Sphinx is a sculpture that can also be found at the city of Giza near the Great Pyramid. It has the body of a lion and the head of a man. Scientists are unsure how old it is and who it was built for, but some people think it was built before the Great Pyramid. The Sphinx is sometimes seen as a mythical monster because of the Ancient Greek story known as the Riddle of the Sphinx, however that image does not exist in Kemetic mythology. Instead the Sphinx was seen as a respected guardian that represented the relationship between humans and gods. The name Sphinx is a Greek name, the true Kemetic name for the Sphinx is Her-Em-Ahket.

The ancient Greeks are given credit for the creation of the tall, slender, stone structure known

 as the obelisk. A type of obelisk can be found in Washington D.C. in the form of the Washington Monument. An obelisk is actually a copy of a Kemetic structure called a Teken that was built in Kemet 3,200 years before the one in Washington D.C. Tekens were often placed outside of temples and religious buildings and often represented resurrection and rebirth after death.

The temples, monuments, and tombs that were erected in Kemet were built to last and withstand the test of time because they were more than just buildings; they were memorials to those people and gods that played such a central role in their everyday lives. The Kemetic people were master architects and builders whose advanced mathematical abilities allowed them to construct some of the most amazing stone structures the world has ever seen.

Show What You Know! – Kemetic Architectural Achievements

Reading for Understanding

1. Why were the pyramids built?

   _____

   _____

   _____

2. Describe the steps that it took to build a pyramid.

   _____

   _____

   _____

3. Describe the first pyramid ever built. Who designed it and who was it built for?

   _____

   _____

   _____

4. Describe the Kemetic Sphinx.

   _____

   _____

   _____

5. What is a Teken?

   _____

   _____

   _____

Take it to the Next Level

1. Research one of the structures built by the Kemetic people and write a one page report about what you discovered.
2. Create a comic strip where you describe the steps it took to build a pyramid. The comic strip should be at least six scenes long and include captions that describe each scene.
3. Research one of the structures built by the Kemetic people and build your own model.

Cross-curricular Connections

Math: The Great Pyramid was built using 2.5 million limestone blocks. Each block weighs 2.5 tons. One ton is equivalent to 2000 pounds. Calculate how much the Great Pyramid weighs in total pounds.

Science: Research the connection between the Pyramids of Giza and the stars that make up the "belt" in the constellation Orion.

Kemetic Religion

The religion practiced in Ancient Kemet was very different from what we know about religion today. This was due to the fact that their religion was infused into every aspect of their daily lives, not something that they practiced on certain days of the week or times of day. There was no particular founder or prophet, and no single book that they read from. Their religion was part of who they were. The people of Ancient Kemet were monotheistic, which is the belief in only one God, however many people believed that they were polytheistic, which is the belief in many gods, because the one God they believed in took many forms. Their religion influenced everything they did, from how they interacted with each other to how they built their pyramids.

Everything the people did in their daily lives had to do with pleasing the gods and living a good life so they could go on to the Afterlife. The Afterlife was the life in which Ancient Kemetic people believed they would go to if they did everything they were supposed to and followed the rules of their religion; it was similar to the Christian concept of Heaven. In order to get to the afterlife you had to follow the rules of MA'AT.

MA'AT was to Kemetic people what the Ten Commandments are to people who practice Judaism or Christianity, except instead of ten rules to follow, the Kemetic people had to follow forty-two! Besides being rules that people had to follow, MA'AT was also the name of one of the most respected goddesses. She stood for truth, justice, and balance in the world. People tried to live their lives according to the rules of MA'AT. Some of these rules included:

- "I have not committed sin."
- "I have not told lies."
- "I have not cursed."
- "I have not been an eavesdropper."

The Kemetic people believed that when a person died, their soul went to the Underworld. The Underworld was not a place filled with fire or the Devil, but was instead similar to a waiting room where you sat waiting for your soul to be judged. When you journeyed there, you would meet Osiris the god of the Underworld. Osiris was what the Greeks called him when they adopted Kemetic culture, however the Kemetic people called him Ausar. He would judge you by performing the "Weighing of the Heart Ceremony" where he would take your heart and placing it on a scale and weigh it against a feather.

The feather stood for the forty-two rules of MA'AT, and the heart stood for all of the good and bad deeds that you did in your life. If your heart was lighter than the feather then you led a good life and would pass on to the Afterlife. If your heart was heavier than the feather then you lived a bad life and your soul would be eaten by the god Ammit and you would cease to exist.

The "Weighing of the Heart Ceremony" was the driving force behind everything Kemetic people did. They wanted to live extraordinarily good and decent lives to please their gods and make sure their souls were able to transition into the Afterlife. It was the main motivation of their entire society, and one of the main reasons why the Kemetic civilization lasted for over four thousand years.

Show What You Know! – Kemetic Religion

Reading for Understanding

1. What does monotheistic mean? What does polytheistic mean?

    _____

    _____

    _____

2. Why does Ancient Egyptian religion not have a name?

    _____

    _____

    _____

3. Describe the Underworld. How was it different than the Afterlife?

    _____

    _____

    _____

4. What was MA'AT?

    _____

    _____

    _____

5. Describe the "Weighing of the Heart Ceremony".

    _____

    _____

    _____

Take it to the Next Level

1. Draw a comic strip that describes the Weighing of the Heart Ceremony. The comic strip must be at least six scenes long and include captions that describe each scene.
2. Research the forty-two rules of MA'AT and write a paragraph describing if you think you could follow the rules or not? Explain why or why not. Which rules would be the easiest to follow? Which would be the hardest? Why?
3. Pretend you are in the Underworld being judged by Ausar/Osiris on your conduct while you were living. Create a dialogue between the two of you as he goes through the forty-two rules of MA'AT and discuss and explain why you followed some but did not follow others.

Cross-curricular Connections

Math: The average human heart weighs about 11 ounces. The average feather weighs .00028 ounces. How many feathers would it take to weigh as much as one heart?

Science: Research the Kemetic process embalming and burying dead bodies and compare it to our modern-day process of embalming and burial.

The Moors

The Moors, black Muslims from the area of Morocco in North Africa, had a highly advanced civilization that expanded their empire out of Africa, and brought it across the Mediterranean Sea, into the European countries of Spain and Portugal. Before the arrival of the Moors in 711 ACE, Europe was in the midst of a one thousand year cultural, intellectual, and technological stagnation. Due to the influence of the almost eight hundred-year Moorish rule of Spain, Europe was able to emerge from the "Dark Ages" with the tools needed to help advance their society.

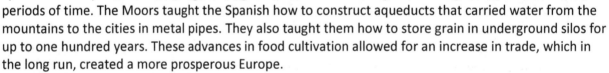

In Europe, during the 8th century, when the Moors arrived, the vast majority of the population was completely illiterate. When the Moors took over, one of the first things they did was to establish a system of universal schooling that allowed everyone to receive an education. At the height of Moorish rule in Spain, they had established seventeen universities, while the rest of the entire continent only had two. In addition, the Moors built over seventy public libraries in Spain, where as the rest of Europe did not contain any. It wasn't until scholars from Paris and Oxford visited the libraries established by the Moors in Spain, did public libraries begin to pop up in other parts of Europe. This notion of free access to information and education radically changed European society, and was directly responsible for them moving out of the "Dark Ages" and into the Renaissance.

Not only did the Moors bring changes to how people obtained an education, but they also drastically changed what types of food people had access to. Moors introduced several different foods to the European diet that did not previously exist, like asparagus, oranges, lemons, peaches, apricots, figs, sugar cane, dates, ginger, and rice. Europeans at the time of Moorish rule in Spain had a very limited knowledge of irrigation and how to store grain for long periods of time. The Moors taught the Spanish how to construct aqueducts that carried water from the mountains to the cities in metal pipes. They also taught them how to store grain in underground silos for up to one hundred years. These advances in food cultivation allowed for an increase in trade, which in the long run, created a more prosperous Europe.

The social and cultural changes that the Moors brought to Spain had just as much impact on their society as the changes in agriculture and education. For instance, daily, (or even weekly, and in some cases monthly) bathing was not the norm in Europe during the "Dark Ages". However, when the Moors took over, they established public bath houses and encouraged daily washing of the body; they even introduced the idea of toothpaste, as well as deodorant. The Moors also altered the way European cities looked and functioned. In the Spanish capital city of Cordoba, where five hundred thousand people lived, they established fifty hospitals, street lighting, paved roads, running water, all of which would not exist in the rest of Europe for another one hundred years.

Europe is often heralded as the center for intellectual and cultural achievement in the world due to their achievements during the Renaissance and Enlightenment periods. However, none of those accomplishments would have been possible if it wasn't for the influence the Moors had on their society. Public access to information, improved diet and hygiene, and numerous scientific advances, all brought by the Moors over the course of eight hundred years, made it possible for Europe to crawl out of their cultural and intellectual paralysis, and make their presence known on the world stage.

Show What you Know! – The Moors

Reading for Understanding

1. Where were the Moors from and what areas of Europe did they conquer?

   _____

   _____

   _____

2. How did the Moors change people's access to education and information in Europe?

   _____

   _____

   _____

3. What were some of the foods that the Moors brought with them from Africa?

   _____

   _____

   _____

4. What cultural and social improvements did the Moors bring with them to Europe?

   _____

   _____

   _____

5. For how many years did the Moors rule Spain?

   _____

   _____

   _____

Take it to the Next Level

1. Create a poem that describes the impact that the Moors had on European society.
2. Write a fictional short story about what you think Europe would be like today if the Moors had never taken over their society.
3. Draw a picture of what you imagine Spain looked like before the Moors ruled and what it looked like after they left.

Cross-curricular Connections

Math: Research Moorish contributions to mathematics, including the concepts of algebra, our modern number system, and the concept of zero.

Science: Research how ancient aqueducts (like the ones the Moors used) worked, and how they are different from modern aqueducts.

Early West African Civilizations

There is a widely held belief that Africa has never produced any great civilizations or has had any significant impact on the world history whatsoever. This belief is sometimes referred to as the "Dark Continent" stereotype. It is a racist stereotype that tries to make Africans look like savages who have no culture and have contributed nothing to the progress of humankind. The stereotype is false; Africa has given birth to hundreds of civilizations, without which the world would most likely not have progressed past the stone age.

Africa's most famous civilization is Ancient Kemet (Egypt) that lasted from approximately 3200 BCE to 30 BCE. Kemet created the world's first religion, writing, schools, and had amazing architecture like the pyramids and Sphinx. Some other great civilizations that existed in Africa hundreds of years ago were Ancient Ghana, Ancient Mali, and Songhai.

Ancient Ghana lasted from about 300 ACE to 1203 ACE. Ghana is most known for its huge amounts of gold. People would come from all over Africa and Europe to trade with Ghana for its gold. In exchange for their gold, the people of Ancient Ghana would often seek out salt to trade. Africans discovered that salt could be used to keep meat fresh, and since this was centuries before the invention of the refrigerator, it was a life changing discovery! Salt was so important to them that they believed it had an equal value to gold!

Ancient Mali lasted from about 1200 ACE to almost 1500 ACE. As the empire of Ghana began to decline, the rulers of Mali used it as an opportunity to expand their territory and take over Ghana's gold and salt trade. Ancient Mali is most well known for their powerful rulers. Their first ruler was called Sundiata and the story of how he came to power was the inspiration for the movie *The Lion King*. The most famous ruler of Ancient Mali was Mansa Musa, who is known for being the richest person in the history of the world! Mansa Musa was a Muslim and according to his religion, he had to make a special trip to the holy land of Mecca at least once in his lifetime. When he made his trip, he took 72,000 people, including 12,000 slaves, each of whom carried 4 pounds of gold, 80 camels that each carried 300 pounds of gold, and 500 hundred servants that rode ahead of him, each one carrying a 10-pound gold staff. In addition, he traveled with 24,000 pounds of gold that he used when he went to restaurants, markets, and shops. He also gave out 20,000 pieces of gold to the poor in every town in which he stopped. He gave out so much gold as he traveled that he caused the value of gold to become almost worthless in three major cities that he visited.

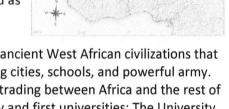

Songhai was the last and one of the most powerful of the ancient West African civilizations that lasted from 1460 ACE to 1591 ACE. It is known most for its amazing cities, schools, and powerful army. The most famous of its cities was Timbuktu. It was the center for trading between Africa and the rest of the world. It was also where you could find one of the world's only and first universities: The University of Sankore.

Learning about these great ancient African civilizations not only offers the proper perspective of the impact that African people have had on human development, but also dispels the myth that Africa is just one big jungle filled with roaming wild animals and dangerous diseases. Africa is populated by thousands of different groups of people, each with its own unique and beautiful history, and the more people learn about them, the more they will grow to appreciate and respect all that African people have accomplished.

Show What You Know! – Early West African Civilizations

Reading for Understanding

1. What does the stereotype of the "Dark Continent" say about Africa and African people?

   _____

   _____

   _____

2. Why was salt so important to the people of Ancient Ghana?

   _____

   _____

   _____

3. Who was Mansa Musa and what did he do?

   _____

   _____

   _____

4. Why was the city of Timbuktu so important?

   _____

   _____

   _____

5. Why is it important for people to learn about these ancient African civilizations?

   _____

   _____

   _____

Take it to the Next Level

1. Write a paragraph that uses evidence from the text that disproves the stereotype of the "Dark Continent".
2. Imagine you are a citizen in one of the towns that Mansa Musa visited on his way to Mecca. Write a journal entry about what you saw and how it impacted you.
3. Using the dates in the text, create a timeline and place Kemet, Ancient Ghana, Ancient Mali, and Songhai in their correct places. Include two facts about each civilization with them on the timeline.

Cross-curricular Connections

Math: Mansa Musa traveled with 12,000 slaves that each carried 4 pounds of gold; 80 camels that each carried 300 pounds of gold; 500 servants that each carried a 10-pound gold staff; and 24,000 pounds of gold used to spend on shopping. How many pounds of gold did he bring with him altogether?

Science: People in West Africa packed their meat in salt to keep it fresh. Research why this process worked, and how it impacted West African society.

Slavery

[1526 ACE - 1888 ACE]

"Is it not enough that we are torn from our country and friends, to toil for your luxury and lust of gain? Must every tender feeling be likewise sacrificed to your avarice?" - Olaudah Equiano

The Beginning of the American Slave Trade

After Columbus landed in the Americas in 1492, Europeans needed people to work their newly acquired land. Europeans did not have experience with farming in this new type of environment so they had to get other people to do it. Since they wanted to make money off of the crops they were growing, they needed to find people who they could get to work without being paid.

People often wondered why Europeans chose Africans as their labor force. Africans were not the Europeans' first choice for enslaved workers. In the beginning, the Europeans tried to use the Native Americans as slaves, but they died too quickly from being overworked and from European diseases like smallpox. So, Europeans turned their attention to Africa for their next source of enslaved labor.

Most Africans were taken from countries in West Africa like Ghana, Sierra Leone, Senegal, and Nigeria, which already had extensive contact with Europeans for hundreds of years through various forms of trade. Therefore, many Africans built up an immunity to European diseases, and did not get as sick from them as the Native Americans did. Africans also knew how to farm different foods than the Native Americans that Europeans thought were important. In addition, Africans already had a system of slavery in Africa that Europeans could exploit, however it was not the same type of system that the Europeans were using. The African system was much different because Africans could gain their freedom back and they had more rights, such as owning property, marrying who they wanted, and helping to make decisions for the village. In the European system, called chattel slavery, Africans had no rights, weren't seen as human, and were to be enslaved for their entire lives as well as the lifetime of all of their descendants.

In order to obtain the Africans they wanted to enslave, sometimes Europeans would attack African villages and steal the people in them. In other instances, some Africans would capture and then sell Africans from neighboring villages into slavery in exchange for things like guns, alcohol or valuable shells. Many of the Africans who did this had no idea the type of life they were selling their own people into because they thought the European form of slavery was the same as their own.

After Africans were captured, they would be forced to walk for miles until they got to the coast, where large ships were waiting to take them to the Americas. Before they could get on the ships, they were made to wait in slave castles. In these castles, that doubled as prisons for the Africans, men and women were separated into large rooms that could hold up to 600 people. There they had to wait, at times for up to a year, with limited food, water, and facilities for personal hygiene. While they were held captive, many died from starvation, dehydration, disease, and the abuse they suffered at the hands of the Europeans which included assault, torture, and rape. Once the Africans were chosen to be transported over to the New World, they would pass through a door that led out of the castle and on to large ships that were waiting for them, this door was called "The Door of No Return", as it was the last time any of them would ever be on African soil ever again.

The trip the Africans were then forced to take across the Atlantic Ocean to North and South America was known as the Middle Passage. The trip lasted up to three months and was the most horrible experience the Africans had ever encountered. Africans were usually put into the bottom of the ship where they were kept for the majority of the trip. Hundreds of Africans were crammed into small sitting spaces that were about 16 inches wide and 3 feet high, or made to lie down on rough wooden boards. They were usually chained together with heavy iron shackles that cut into their flesh to restrict

23

their movement. If they had to go to the bathroom or vomit, they had to do it where they were sitting or lying. The Africans were given very little food or water which caused many to die of starvation and malnutrition, which resulted in about one third of the captives dying on the journey. Sometimes Africans would be allowed outside for exercise, when this happened many white sailors would rape the black women, while the men, powerless in their chains, were forced to watch. The process was repeated thousands of times over the course of the hundreds of years that Europeans enslaved African people.

Africans did not meekly submit to the will of the Europeans. Many Africans did anything they could to resist and fight back against being put into slavery. Many fought hard before they even left Africa. Once they were on the ship, some tried to jump

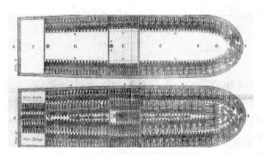

overboard and swim back to their homeland. Some would commit suicide or kill those they loved so they wouldn't have to go through the horrors of being a slave. Some refused to eat, and tried to starve themselves. Others tried to get weapons that were on the ship and fight the white sailors. Unfortunately, most attempts to take over the ships were unsuccessful.

Millions of Africans were stolen from their homeland to be forced into the barbaric system of slavery the Europeans had waiting for them in the Americas. However, there were millions more who did not make it to the New World, whose journey ended in their villages, or in the slave castles, or at the bottom of the Atlantic Ocean. The story of slavery is one of the most horrific events that ever happened to a group of people anywhere, and unfortunately this story lasted for over four hundred years.

Show What You Know! – The Beginning of the American Slave Trade

Reading for Understanding

1. Why did Europeans need other people to work their new lands in the Americas?

   _____

   _____

   _____

2. Why did Europeans decide to use Africans as slaves? Give at least two reasons.

   _____

   _____

   _____

3. What was the difference between the type of slavery Africans used and the type of slavery Europeans used?

   _____

   _____

   _____

4. Describe what slave castles were like in 2-3 sentences.

   _____

   _____

   _____

5. What was the Middle Passage?

   _____

   _____

   _____

Take it to the Next Level

1. Based on what you have read, write a poem, song, or rap that describes the enslavement process African people went through.
2. Draw a mural dedicated to the African men and women who died during the process of enslavement. Be sure to include at least 5 elements from the text in the mural.
3. Think from the perspective of either an African who has been stolen, or an African whose family has been taken from the village, and write a journal entry that describes what you imagine they went through.

Cross-curricular Connections

Math: If there was an average of 400 captured Africans on each slave ship and there were approximately 54,000 trips made that transported Africans to the Americas, but about a total of 1.5 million of them died during the Middle Passage, about how many Africans actually made it to the Americas alive?

Science: Disease killed many Africans while being transported on the Middle Passage. Research the following diseases that caused most of the deaths on the slave ships and determine their causes, their symptoms, and how they can be cured or prevented: Dysentery, scurvy, measles, and smallpox.

The Life of Enslaved Africans in North America

Most of the ships that held the Africans usually landed in the northern part of the United States in places like Boston and New York City. For the Africans that

survived the Middle Passage, another kind of savagery and violence awaited them. Once they were taken off the ships, they were forced into cages and waited to be sold off to white people.

When it was time to be sold, Africans were stripped down naked and forced on to auction blocks, where they were poked, prodded, inspected and then sold to the highest bidder like a piece of merchandise. Once they were sold, enslaved Africans were branded on their back using a red-hot iron with the symbol or logo of their new owner. At this point, families that came over together were often forcibly separated and sold to different owners, never to see each other again.

The first group of Africans brought to North America came in 1619 in Jamestown, Virginia. These first Africans were not necessarily slaves, but then again, they weren't necessarily free either; they were considered indentured servants. Indentured servants were people who were required to work for a period of two to seven years in order to buy their freedom or pay off some sort of debt. At this time, the majority of workers, both black and white, were indentured servants. Whites were usually indentured servants to pay off what it cost them to travel from Europe to America. Most indentured servants died from various diseases and being overworked before they earned their freedom as their owners wanted to get the most out of them while they still could.

As more and more Africans began to be used for slave labor in the Caribbean islands, the British followed this example and began to import more Africans to be used as slaves in North America. In addition, white people found other ways to pay off their debt and become successful members of society and did not need to be indentured servants any more. Soon, indentured servitude was exchanged for the system of chattel slavery. Chattel Slavery was when enslaved people and their descendants become property of their owners for life.

Most Africans were forced to work on either a small farm or a large plantation. A plantation was an extremely large farm that required hundreds of people to work it. There were some whites who owned hundreds, even thousands of Africans and they lived and worked on huge farms called plantations. Most plantations farmed either tobacco, rice, indigo or cotton that would be sold for profit domestically or overseas. Interestingly, most white people did not own slaves because they could not afford them. Those that could afford it had small farms and owned fewer than 5 slaves. In these cases, the slave owners would often work the land along with their enslaved workers.

Life on a plantation was very difficult for enslaved people. The majority of enslaved Africans were agricultural workers who labored in large fields and were made to work from sunup to sundown. They were allowed a couple of breaks for food and rest and were often given Sunday off so they could attend church. African men also held some skilled occupations on a plantation such as carpenter, blacksmith, tanner, shoe maker, and weaver. When African women were not working the fields, they could also be weavers and domestic servants where they would cook, wash, clean and take care of the white children.

Most enslaved Africans lived in small log cabins away from the "big house", which was where  the white family lived. They usually had dirt floors, roofs made of straw or wood, brick fire places, and few, if any windows. Most cabins did not have a lot of furniture, planks of wood or straw as a bed, and wooden crates for seating and storage. In the summer, enslaved men wore a range of clothing, which included roughly made pants, shirts and hats. For women in the summer they also wore a range of just a skirt to a full-length dress and handkerchiefs on their heads. Children were not given any clothes and were naked in the summer until the age of puberty. In the winter, slave owners would sometimes give them one article of heavier woolen clothing, and possibly a pair of cheap leather shoes.

Corn, yams, and salt pork (similar to large chunks of bacon) were the main foods in an enslaved person's life. Occasionally they would catch fish, or raise chickens and rabbits. On some plantations, when they were done with their own work for the day, enslaved Africans were allowed to tend to their own gardens that had vegetables such as cabbage, collard greens, turnips, and black-eyed peas.

Contrary to popular belief, slavery existed in the Northern part of the country for several centuries. Life in the north was completely different due to the larger number of white workers, lack of suitable land for growing crops, and a heavier focus on industry. In the north, black people were only 4.5% of the population compared to the south, in which blacks made up 40% of the population. Most enslaved Africans in the north were farmers like they were in the south however most of them worked and lived with their owners on small farms. Other jobs for those enslaved in the north were shopkeepers, messengers, house servants, and general city workers. Northern blacks tended to have more rights than southern blacks due to the heavier stress on religion in the north as well as their fewer numbers which meant less of a need for security. Because of their small numbers, frequent isolation from others of African descent, and close association with their owners, blacks enslaved in the north usually had fewer opportunities to preserve their African heritage.

While each state, county and even plantation had varying ways of carrying out the system of slavery, what is known is that regardless of location, slavery in North America was a brutal, dehumanizing practice that forced millions of people to live in appalling conditions.

Show What You Know! – The Life of Enslaved Africans in North America

Reading for Understanding

1. What were indentured servants and how were they different than people in chattel slavery?

    _____

    _____

    _____

2. What kind of work did enslaved people have to do on plantations?

    _____

    _____

    _____

3. What was the Big House?

    _____

    _____

    _____

4. Describe what a slave cabin might look like.

    _____

    _____

    _____

5. How was life for an enslaved person in the North different for one in the South?

    _____

    _____

    _____

Take it to the Next Level

1. Write a paragraph about what it was like to be an enslaved person. In your paragraph make sure to include the following words: **sold, indentured servant, chattel, plantation, farm, forced.**
2. Draw what you think a typical scene would look like on a plantation. In your illustration include the Big House, fields for crops, slave cabins, and enslaved people working or eating.
3. Create a two circle Venn Diagram that compares and contrasts slavery in the south against slavery in the north.

Cross-curricular Connections

Math: Mr. Johnson has a plantation that is divided up into three different sections. The section for the big house is 230 feet by 150 feet. The section for the slave cabins is 15 feet by 75 feet. The section for growing crops is 900 feet by 650 feet. What is the total area of Mr. Johnson's plantation?

Science: The Cotton Gin was an invention created by Eli Whitney in 1793 to help make picking cotton easier. Research how the Cotton Gin worked, and if it made life easier or harder for enslaved black people.

Resistance to Slavery

Since the beginning of the slave trade, African people resisted and fought back against the system that sought to take away their families, culture, homeland, lives, and humanity. Africans fought back on the African continent, on the ships that took them to the Americas, and on the plantations. There were two main types of resistance to slavery: overt and covert. Overt Resistance was when Africans fought back violently and out in the open for everyone to see. Covert Resistance was when African did things to resist and fight back secretly, usually without many people knowing.

The fear of punishment and death was always looming over the heads of enslaved people, but this could not stop many of them from fighting back in their own subtle way. When using Covert Resistance "house slaves" were well known for resisting against their "owners" by putting ground up glass or poison in their food. "Field slaves" would often break tools, kill livestock, and burn down barns and fields as a way of getting a couple of hours or days of rest from their work. Enslaved Africans of all kinds sometimes resisted by faking injury or sickness to get a break from the work that they had to do.

One of the most important ways that Africans covertly resisted slavery was by trying to hold on to their African culture and reject the culture that the European Americans were trying to force on them. They would often meet in secret at night and play the drums, which had been outlawed in most places. They would tell stories from their homeland in their natural languages and perform their own rituals and traditions that they had practiced in Africa. All religions that Africans practiced in Africa were outlawed, including all indigenous religions and Islam, so Africans would often sneak away at night and practice their religions while during the day pretending to be Christians like their owners.

Many Africans were fed up with the constant beatings, rape, poor living and working conditions, and general mistreatment at the hands of white people. Many African men and women overtly fought back against their white oppressors, sometimes severely injuring or even killing them. Sometimes this resistance was a spontaneous reaction to some sort of abuse, however at other times it was a planned action, involving groups of Africans with the goal of killing the owner and freeing everyone on the plantation.

If caught, resistance of any kind was certain to carry severe consequences, so Africans who chose to resist overtly knew that they were risking death by openly fighting back. Some enslaved Africans preferred to risk death rather than be a slave any longer and many openly fought back against their "masters" by trying to harm or kill them and other whites in their quest for freedom.

Show What You Know! – Resistance to Slavery

Reading for Understanding

1. What is Overt Resistance?

   _____

   _____

   _____

2. What is Covert Resistance?

   _____

   _____

   _____

3. Give two examples of overt resistance.

   _____

   _____

   _____

4. Give two examples of covert resistance.

   _____

   _____

   _____

5. Based on your opinion, which do you think would have been more effective: overt or covert resistance? Explain your answer.

   _____

   _____

   _____

Take it to the Next Level

1. Imaging you are an enslaved person trying to convince other people to join you in resisting. Write a dialogue that shows what the conversation would have been like. Include which type of resistance you plan on doing, as well as the benefits and drawbacks to each type of resistance.
2. Research one of the following rebellions and write a one-page report on your findings: The Stono Rebellion; The German Coast Rebellion; The Amistad Rebellion.
3. Write a play that centers around a group of Africans meeting at night to plan how they were going to fight back against their slave owners.

Cross-curricular Connections

Math: If there is a slave ship carrying 375 Africans, along with 28 boxes of axes, and if each box contains 13 axes, how many Africans would not have axes if they broke free and used the axes to resist against the Europeans?

Science: Many Africans would choose to run away from the plantations as a form of resistance. Research which season would be the best in which to escape. Create a chart for each season, describing the benefits and drawbacks for running away during each one.

Important African Americans Who Resisted Slavery

Harriet Tubman

Harriet Tubman was born as an enslaved person around 1820 in Maryland. She escaped slavery in 1849 and fled to Philadelphia in the North where slavery was

outlawed. She became part of the Underground Railroad movement that helped sneak enslaved people off of plantations and transport them to the North where they could be free. Harriet Tubman returned to the South nineteen different times and freed over 300 enslaved people. When the Civil War started, she joined the side of the Union (the North) and became a spy for them. Her efforts helped them win several battles against the Confederacy (the South).

Denmark Vesey

Denmark Vesey, whose birth name was Telemanque (TELL-A-MAN-KAY), was born in West Africa around 1767. He was captured when he was a young boy, and sold into slavery in the islands of the

Caribbean and then to the Charleston, South Carolina. In 1800, he won a $1500 prize in the lottery and bought his own freedom and opened a carpentry shop. He became a very successful carpenter and was respected by both blacks and whites. At this time, he started reading anti-slavery books, which led him to start planning a slave revolt. His plan was to gather nine thousand enslaved and free Africans on July 14, 1822 and take over the entire town of Charleston, South Carolina. His plan was to raid the armory, steal all of the weapons, and give them to all of the black people in the town and to have them kill all of the slave owners. Another black person, who was looking to get favors from the whites in the town, betrayed Vesey and told the whites about his plan. Vesey was caught and hung in the town for trying to overthrow slavery.

Gabriel Prosser

Gabriel Prosser was an enslaved person living in Virginia. He was taught how to read and write and was a very skilled craftsman, which allowed him to be hired out to different plantations to work. During his travel to various plantations, he got to meet a lot of people, both black and white, who were against the idea of slavery. It was after exchanging ideas with many of these people that he got the idea of starting a revolt. He built a secret army of enslaved people from all over Virginia and planned to take over the capital of Richmond, Virginia. Prosser planned to kidnap the governor and hold him hostage in exchange for the freedom for all the enslaved people involved in the revolt. Before he could carry out his revolt, one of the enslaved Africans he was working with told one of the slave owners and the army was called. The revolt was halted before it could begin. Gabriel and twenty-six other enslaved Africans were executed as a result of the planned revolt.

Show What You Know! – Important African Americans Who Resisted Slavery

Reading For Understanding

1. Describe three important details about Harriet Tubman's life.

_____

_____

_____

2. What caused Denmark Vesey to want to resist against slavery?

_____

_____

_____

3. Why did Gabriel Prosser's revolt fail?

_____

_____

_____

4. What are two things that each of the above people have in common?

_____

_____

_____

5. What was unique about each of them?

_____

_____

_____

Take it to the Next Level

1. Create a three circle Venn Diagram and compare and contrast Harriet Tubman, Gabriel Prosser, and Denmark Vesey.
2. Research the Underground Railroad and write a one-page paper describing what you have learned.
3. Research what Harriet Tubman went through as she was escorting enslaved people to freedom. Write a fictional story based on her experiences.

Cross-curricular Connections

Math: Harriet Tubman had to travel 500 miles when she was transporting enslaved people from Maryland all the way to Toronto, Canada. If she traveled 17 miles a day how many days would it take for them to make it to Canada?

Science: Enslaved people led very stressful lives, especially if they planned on running away or resisting. To deal with stress, the body produces a chemical called cortisol. Research the positive and negative aspects of cortisol on the human body.

Nat Turner

Nat Turner was born on October 2, 1800 in South Hampton County, Virginia. His mother's name was Nancy, however not much is known about her. Many people thought Turner was special because from a very young age he would often describe things that had happened before he was born. Some people even called him a prophet. When he was a child, Nat was allowed to learn to read and write by his owners, mostly so he could learn about the Bible and Christianity. Because of that, Nat became very religious and was often seen reading the Bible and praying. He also believed heavily in signs from God, as well as divine intervention, which would play a huge role in his life in the future.

In 1825, he had a vision of a bloody fight between black and white spirits. Three years later, he said a spirit came to him and said "the Serpent was loosened, and Christ had laid down the yoke he had borne for the sins of men, and that I should take it on and fight against the Serpent, for the time was fast approaching when the first should be last and the last should be first." Turner took this as a sign that he "should arise and prepare myself and slay my enemies with their own weapons." In February of 1831, Nat witnessed a solar eclipse which he believed was the sign for him to rise up against the white slave owners. He started to recruit other enslaved people that he could trust and began planning their rebellion.

On August 21, 1831, Nat Turner began his revolt by killing the white people on the plantation where he worked, freeing the slaves and securing more weapons. Nat Turner and his fellow rebels moved from plantation to plantation killing as many whites as they could and gaining more participants for their insurrection. They secured some guns but decided to use axes, hatchets, knives and blunt instruments instead so that they would not alert the white people that they were coming. Nat's group of more than 70 enslaved and freed blacks descended on the plantations in the area, killing nearly 60 white men, women, and children. Turner's plan was to get to the armory in Jerusalem, Virginia in order to secure more weapons and eventually free all the blacks in the entire area. When they arrived at the armory, they were met by an armed white militia three times their size who attacked them, killing, wounding and capturing many of Nat's comrades.

When he realized that he could not defeat the white militia, Nat retreated into the woods. After a massive manhunt, he was eventually captured on October 30, 1831. When he was brought to trial, Nat Turner pled not guilty because he said he believed he was doing God's work. Turner was found guilty and was put to death by hanging on November 11, 1831. After he was hung, "Turner was skinned to supply such souvenirs as purses, his flesh made into grease, and his bones divided as trophies to be handed down as heirlooms."

Nat Turner's rebellion was one of the largest and most successful slave revolts to ever take place in the United States. His actions had ripple effects on both black and white people throughout the entire country. After Nat Turner's rebellion was defeated, many whites were scared and angry and began attacking and killing innocent slaves and free blacks. In addition, many laws were passed in states throughout the south that made life for blacks even more restricted. One law in particular made it illegal for blacks to be taught to read and write. The United States would be forever transformed because of Nat Turner and his fight for freedom.

Show What You Know! – Nat Turner

Reading For Understanding

1. Why did many people think Nat Turner was special?

   _____

   _____

   _____

2. What kinds of visions or "signs" did Nat receive? How did those signs influence his actions?

   _____

   _____

   _____

3. What was Nat's plan and what was the outcome of the rebellion?

   _____

   _____

   _____

4. Why did Nat plead "not guilty" to the crimes he was accused of?

   _____

   _____

   _____

5. What impact did Nat Turner's rebellion have on the rest of the country?

   _____

   _____

   _____

Take it to the Next Level

1. Write a letter to Nat Turner where you express your thoughts on his rebellion and ask any questions that you have for him about what he did or what he went through. Then respond to that letter as Nat Turner in the way that you think he would based on what you have learned about him.
2. Many of the laws that were put into place after Nat Turner was killed were called the Slave Codes. Research ten of the Slave Codes and list them in order of least cruel to most cruel.
3. Create a comic strip about Nat Turner's rebellion. The comic strip should be at least six scenes long and each scene should contain captions that describe that scene.

Cross-curricular Connections

Math: If Nat had about 70 rebels with him, and were met with a force three times that size when they went to the armory, how many men were waiting for them when they arrived there?

Science: One of the signs that influenced Nat Turner the most was the solar eclipse. Research how a solar eclipse occurs and when the next solar eclipse will take place.

Toussaint L'Ouverture and the Haitian Revolution

Francois Toussaint, later known as Toussaint L'Ouverture, was born on May 20, 1743. He was the grandson of a West African king, however his family was sold into slavery and sent to the Caribbean. Toussaint was enslaved on the island of Hispaniola, which would later be called Haiti and the Dominican Republic.

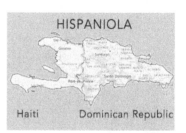

As an enslaved person, he was afforded the rare opportunity to be able to learn to read and write. His tastes in books ranged from the classic philosophers to Catholic texts. His expert knowledge and skill in the growing and use of medicinal plants, as well as horsemanship afforded him the opportunity to be granted the position of chief steward on the plantation on which he served. Toussaint was later granted his freedom around 1776, but continued to work for his former owner. In 1782, he married Suzanne Baptist and they had 3 children together.

On August 22, 1791 enslaved Africans on the western half of the island started a revolt during which many whites were killed due to how poorly they had been treating their slaves. Initially, Toussaint did not involve himself in the revolt. He was almost 50 years old when the revolt took place, and he also had a family that he wanted to make sure were safe. Toussaint finally committed to participating in the revolution, but only after he moved his family, as well as his former owner to a safe distance outside of the city.

HISPANIOLA

Haiti   Dominican Republic

Toussaint joined the rebels who had allied themselves with the Spanish who were helping with the overthrow of the French on the island. He started out as a doctor and a soldier but soon rose in the ranks and was given a battalion of his own troops to command. As he was leading his new troops, he adopted the last name L'Ouverture, which is French for "opening the way". One of Toussaint's most trusted lieutenants, and one of the most important people in the revolution, was an escaped slave named Jean-Jacques Dessalines.

As a way of trying to gain the allegiance of the non-revolting black population in Hispaniola, the French decided to grant freedom and citizenship to all blacks in all of their colonies around the globe. This strategy worked to a degree, as Toussaint promptly switched sides and began fighting with the French to push the Spanish out of Hispaniola. With the Spanish gone, Toussaint was the leading political and military figure on the island. He experienced some resistance from the mixed blacks who wanted to reinstitute slavery, but they were defeated with the help of Dessalines' army.

Once the last rebellion was put down, Toussaint ruled the entire island. He created a constitution, abolished slavery, and made himself Governor-General for life. As ruler, he improved agricultural and economic conditions, created trade agreements with the British and Americans, and made significant improvements in the conditions of workers on the island.

When Napoleon Bonaparte took over France in 1799, Toussaint feared that he would reinstitute slavery. Instead, he confirmed Toussaint's role as a colonial governor and agreed not to bring slavery back. The French still had a presence in the eastern side of the island and Toussaint wanted to get rid of them so he marched with his army and fought the remaining French troops and took the land from them. As a response, Napoleon sent an army of 20,000 troops to regain control of the entire island.

Toussaint fought for several months, but whites and the mixed blacks on the island sided with Napoleon and Toussaint was overwhelmed. As a ploy to get him out in the open, the French invited Toussaint to a meeting to discuss a peace treaty. At that meeting he was captured and then transferred to France where he was tortured and starved. Toussaint L'Ouverture succumbed to his injuries and died on April 7, 1803.

Soon after Toussaint's death, Dessalines took command of the remaining troops still loyal to Toussaint and rebelled against the French. The French were defeated and in 1804, Dessalines proclaimed independence for the island and named himself its emperor. He renamed the island Haiti, which is a word that means land of high mountains in the island's indigenous language. Haiti became the first independent black republic in the world.

Show What You Know! – Toussaint L'Ouverture and the Haitian Revolution

Reading for Understanding

1. Why did a revolt start on the island of Hispaniola?

   _____

   _____

   _____

2. Why did Toussaint initially not join in the revolt?

   _____

   _____

   _____

3. What did the French do to gain the support of black people on the island? Did it work?

   _____

   _____

   _____

4. What sorts of things did Toussaint do once he was in control of the island?

   _____

   _____

   _____

5. Describe what happened between Toussaint and Napoleon.

   _____

   _____

   _____

Take it to the Next Level

1. Imagine the Haitian Revolution happened in modern times. Create a text conversation between Toussaint and Napoleon that illustrates what the two could have talked about after Napoleon took over France.
2. Today Haiti is one of the poorest countries in the world. Research what has happened to Haiti since their independence that has caused them to decline economically.
3. Create a "wanted" poster that the French might have created as they were looking for Toussaint L'Ouverture. On the poster include an illustration of what Toussaint looked like, at least 4 facts about his life and what crimes they believed he committed.

Cross-curricular Connections

Math: If the island of Hispaniola covers an area of 29,418 square miles and the United States covers an area of about 3,800,000 square miles, how many times can Hispaniola fit into the United States?
Science: Toussaint L'Ouverture was an expert at the use of plants and herbs to cure ailments and diseases. Research what plants can cure the following health problems: headache, upset stomach, sore muscles or joints, and poor eyesight.

Colonization and Independence in Africa

[1884 ACE - 1977 ACE]

"It is a question of creating a new state, as big as possible, and of running it. It is clearly understood that in this project there is no question of granting the slightest political power to the negroes. That would be absurd." - King Leopold II of Belgium

The Berlin Conference

The enslavement of African people had ended in most areas of the world by the end of the 1800s. This was due to many slave revolts and protests from people stating that slavery was wrong and that Africans were human beings who did not deserve to be slaves. The pressure from this new feeling helped to outlaw the system of slavery. However, when slavery ended, it also ended the steady flow of money into the hands of many European leaders. In search of new streams of income, the Europeans turned their attention back to Africa, this time, instead of people, they were interested in the large amounts of natural resources that Africa possessed and wanted to use them to increase their wealth.

This desire for profit led the leaders of the major European countries to meet in Berlin, Germany in 1884 at what became known as the Berlin Conference. At this meeting, without consulting any African leaders, they divided Africa into colonies for the different European countries. A colony is a place (city, state, or country) that is ruled and governed by another group of people who are from a foreign land. Most colonies are extensions of the country that is ruling them, meaning they are made to take on the same culture as the ruling country, they have to pay taxes to the ruling country, and all of the land and resources belong to the ruling country.

It was not easy for the Europeans to colonize an entire continent because Africans did not want to be ruled by other people and they resisted whenever they could. However, the Europeans were very strategic and developed three specific methods for colonizing the different African countries. They were through the use of the military, the missionaries, and manipulation.

The use of the military was the most direct method for trying to make someone else's land a colony. The European countries all had very strong armies and most could overpower any African army simply because the Europeans had guns and African armies did not. When Europeans used the military, they marched into a country and fought the different ethnic groups until they all surrendered and promised to give control of their land to the European country.

Missionaries are people who travel to different places trying to teach and spread the ideas of their religion. Many European countries would send missionaries to Africa and try to convert the people to Christianity. Many Europeans held the belief that the traditional religions practiced by African people were inferior to their own, and that they were saving the souls of the Africans by teaching them Christianity. Converting Africans to Christianity also made it easier for Africans to be colonized. Africans who believed that God, Jesus, angels, and other key figures from the Bible, were white were more likely to allow Europeans to rule them because they equated their whiteness with holiness.

Manipulation means to use someone in an unfair way, usually to your own advantage. This method happened in many different ways; however, the most reliable way was when Europeans found Africans who were greedy and only cared about themselves to betray their countries. They would promise them rewards as long as they helped overthrow the old African government. Once that happened, the Europeans would put that person in power because they knew that person was loyal to Europe and not Africa.

The Europeans at the Berlin Conference created boundary lines between each of their new territories which is how we get our modern country boundaries in Africa. These boundary lines were drawn without consideration of the traditional territories that had been held by the various African ethnic groups for thousands of years. Groups were moved, some were split up, and others were combined with groups they did not get along with. This caused the different ethnic groups to fight with each other and start wars over who was supposed to be living on the land. Throughout all of this, Europeans began taking all of the natural resources that Africa had to offer such as gold, diamonds, rubber, and oil and used them to increase their wealth and power throughout the globe.

Show What You Know! – The Berlin Conference

Reading for Understanding

1. What led Europeans to start colonizing Africa?

    _____

    _____

    _____

2. What was the Berlin Conference?

    _____

    _____

    _____

3. What were the three main methods that Europeans used to colonize Africa?

    _____

    _____

    _____

4. Which of the three methods do you think was most effective and why?

    _____

    _____

    _____

5. What were some effects that colonization had on Africa and African people?

    _____

    _____

    _____

Take it to the Next Level

1. Draw a picture of what you think the Berlin Conference looked like.
2. Draw a picture of what you think each method the Europeans used to colonize Africa looked like.
3. Ethiopia was the only African country not to be colonized by an outside group. Research how Ethiopia was able to stay independent and write a one-page report about what you learned.

Cross-curricular Connections

Math: Britain held Egypt, Sudan, Kenya, Nigeria, Ghana, Sierra Leone, South Africa, Uganda, Botswana, Zambia, and Zimbabwe as colonies. Research each country's total area and determine how much land Britain controlled in Africa.

Science: Research which countries in Africa contain gold, diamonds, and oil.

The Colonization of the Congo

The area that Europeans referred to as the "Congo" actually covers the area now called the Democratic Republic of the Congo (DRC). The land is covered by a thick, dense rainforest, large mountains, and the second longest river in Africa: the Congo River. The amount of land that DRC covers is larger than England, France, Germany, Spain, and Italy combined.

Most of the Congo was unexplored by Europeans because they could not figure out how to make it through the rain forest and past the mountains. So instead they (mainly the French) stayed on the coast which they used to expand their shipping business. It wasn't until the King of Belgium, Leopold II, started to show an interest in the area that the entire Congo was threatened with colonization.

Belgium is a small European country located between Germany, France, and the Netherlands. Compared to the other European countries, Belgium was small and didn't have as much military strength compared to the European countries nearby. This was extremely troubling for Belgium's King Leopold II because he wanted to expand his territory, but knew he couldn't defeat any of his neighbors in battle. So, instead of trying to increase the land around him in Europe, he decided to try and gain more resources for his country by trying to colonize different areas of Africa. When he brought the proposal for colonization to the rest of the government, they rejected his plan for any colonization because they didn't see it as profitable.

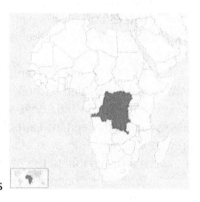

King Leopold did not like being told he couldn't have his colony, so as a response, he created a fake company that he said would be used to help African people get food, fight diseases, etc., which a lot of Europeans supported. He used the money he raised through this company to buy supplies and pay people to go over to the Congo and take the land from the Africans living there. Instead of colonizing the Congo for the country of Belgium, he decided to colonize it as his own personal property and use all of its resources to increase his own personal wealth and status.

> *"It is a question of creating a new state, as big as possible, and of running it. It is clearly understood that in this project there is no question of granting the slightest political power to the negroes. That would be absurd." - King Leopold II*

At first, King Leopold wanted to trade ivory and sugar but that turned out to not be very profitable. Then he found out that in the Congo Rainforest there were thousands of trees that produced liquid latex, which is the material used to make rubber. At the same time in Europe, people had recently discovered how to use rubber to make tires for their bikes and cars. King Leopold knew if he could get as much of the rubber from the Congo as possible and sell it to Europe, he could make a lot of money.

King Leopold told the people he sent to the Congo to do anything and everything they needed to in order to gain possession of the rubber trees. In some cases, he would send his people to negotiate with African chiefs and promise them things in exchange for the rights to their land. In other cases, they would trick the African chiefs by making them sign contracts that were written in languages the Africans couldn't understand, which gave all of their land and resources to Leopold. Any group or village that refused to help harvest the rubber was immediately killed or burned to the ground to show other groups what would happen if they tried to resist. If an individual person refused to gather the rubber, they would be whipped, beaten, or had their wives or children kidnapped until they gave in to the demands of King Leopold. Europeans also brought with them many diseases that the people of the Congo had never experience because they had very little contact with Europeans before colonization. These diseases contributed to the death of millions of Congolese people.

One of the horrific acts King Leopold and his men became well known for was cutting off the hands of African people. King Leopold wanted to make sure that he was making as much money as possible from his new colony, so he made sure that none of the supplies that he bought were wasted. Bullets were especially expensive and his men were known for shooting random animals, trees, and even people for no particular reason. To make sure that they weren't shooting things besides people, Leopold said that for each bullet that a soldier fired from his gun he had to prove that it was used to kill an actual African person by showing the cut off hand of the dead person they killed. Unfortunately, the soldiers continued to waste bullets, but to stay out of trouble they would cut the hands off of innocent Africans who were still living.

After 20 years of colonization, more than 20 million African people had been killed because of the Belgians. News of the horrible things happening in The Congo started to spread around the world. The British and American newspapers exposed King Leopold, and he was forced to give up the Congo as his own personal property. However, instead of allowing the country to become completely independent, it just transferred ownership to the Belgian government.

While The Congo was under Belgian rule very few things improved. They were still being used for their labor and resources; the only difference was that they weren't being killed in large numbers anymore. Over the course of the next 50 years, the Africans pressured the Belgians to grant them independence using guerilla warfare and protests. It was the constant protesting and marching that finally led to the Belgians giving up their colony in 1960 and allowing The Congo to finally become independent.

The crimes committed against the Africans in the Belgian Congo were some of the most horrific the world has ever seen. The death of millions of its people, coupled with the removal of its valuable resources by the Belgians, had a disastrous effect on the country's economic and cultural stability that is still being felt today.

Show What You Know! – The Colonization of the Congo

Reading for Understanding

1. Why was it difficult for Europeans to colonize the Congo?

   _____

   _____

   _____

2. Why did King Leopold want to colonize the Congo?

   _____

   _____

   _____

3. What natural resource did the Congo have that King Leopold wanted most? What was he going to use it for?

   _____

   _____

   _____

4. How were the Africans treated by the Belgians? Give three examples.

   _____

   _____

   _____

5. How did the Congo gain their independence from Belgium?

   _____

   _____

   _____

Take it to the Next Level

1. Create a "wanted" poster for King Leopold II. On the poster include a picture or drawing of what he looked like; three facts about him; and what crimes he has committed.
2. Analyze the quote from King Leopold provided in the text. What do you think he meant?
3. Respond to the prompt: Do you think that modern day Belgium should be held responsible for what happened to the people of the Congo more than one hundred years ago? Explain your answer with examples from the text.

Cross-curricular Connections

Math: If the Congo was under King Leopold's control for 20 years and 20 million Africans died during that time, on average, how many Africans died each year?

Science: What is the process of taking raw rubber from a tree and making it into a tire for a car?

Kenya and Its Fight for Independence

Kenya is a country that is located on the eastern coast of Africa. It is bordered by Tanzania, Uganda, Sudan, Ethiopia, Somalia, and the Indian Ocean. Lake Victoria, Africa's largest lake, creates part of Kenya's southwestern border. Kenya has a very diverse geography which consists of beautiful coast lines with white sand beaches, rich grasslands where many wild animals can be found, as well as the highlands that have a cooler climate, which makes it good for farming.

Kenya's proximity to the Indian ocean made it extremely valuable to Arab traders who were nearby in the Middle East. Over time, many of those Arabs mixed with the black Africans and created a new ethnic group and language called Swahili. Other ethnic groups that lived there were the Maasai and the Kikuyu. Most of the ethnic groups in Kenya were either farmers or herders living in the highlands of Kenya. Ethnic groups in Kenya lived fairly peaceful lives before the Europeans came. The Swahili ethnic group lived mainly on the coast and conducted trade with the Arabs coming in from the Middle East. They traded ivory, wood and unfortunately, slaves; which the Arabs wanted.

After the end of the slave trade, Britain started colonizing large areas of East Africa because of its fertile land and its close proximity to Asia, which was a trading partner of the British. At first, the British only colonized the coastal areas because they wanted to dominate the trading in the region, but soon they realized that Kenya had a lot of fertile land in the highlands and they sent many British settlers there to farm the land. However, a major problem arose: many Africans from the Kikuyu and Maasai ethnic groups were already on the land and had lived there for hundreds of years.

The British chose to favor the people from the Maasai ethnic group who recently had a severe drought and loss of crops and animals. The British promised them lands and positions of power in exchange for their cooperation. Since the Maasai were experiencing hard times, they took the deal, and assisted the British in controlling the other ethnic groups. The British grouped the other ethnic groups into "tribes" and placed them on specific land and made it illegal for them to leave that area. The British began stealing much of the farming land of the Kikuyu ethnic group which forced many of them into poverty and starvation. To "help" them, the British would allow them back onto the land in exchange for them working the farms as cheap labor. In this new British controlled country, blacks were not allowed to own land and could not vote.

At first, the Kenyans tried to reason with the British and attempted to change their policies using political means. A group was formed called the Kikuyu Central Association (KCA) and was led by a man named Jomo Kenyatta. Kenyatta and the KCA tried to get the British to return their land and grant them more rights but since they couldn't vote and had no representatives in government, their strategy failed.

Many Kikuyu people could see that politics were not going to work and were getting angry because of their lack of rights and increasing poverty. They decided to form a military group called the Mau Mau whose goal was to use guerilla warfare to gain back their country. Guerilla warfare is when a small group of fighters uses sneak attacks, hit and run tactics and their knowledge of the local geography, to fight a larger army. For about five years, the Mau Mau waged guerilla war against the British and other Africans who supported the whites. They called for Kenyan independence from the British and gained a lot of support from the majority of the black population.

The Mau Mau were no match for the British military and were almost completely wiped out after about five years of fighting. However, the Mau Mau had produced a feeling of nationalism around the country and gained the support of the people of Kenya and the British knew that they would never be able to govern there peacefully. They granted Kenya the right to have free elections for all citizens, and in 1963 the people of Kenya elected Jomo Kenyatta to be their first independent president, resulting in the end of British rule of Kenya.

Show What You Know! – Kenya and Its Fight For Independence

Reading for Understanding

1. Describe the geography of Kenya in 3-5 sentences.

   _____

   _____

   _____

2. What European group came to colonize Kenya and why?

   _____

   _____

   _____

3. What methods were used to make Kenya a colony?

   _____

   _____

   _____

4. Who were the Mau Mau and what did they do?

   _____

   _____

   _____

5. What led to Kenya gaining their independence?

   _____

   _____

   _____

Take it to the Next Level

1. Imagine you are the British trying to colonize Kenya. Create a dialogue of you trying to convince the Kikuyu and Maasai to allow you to take control of their land.
2. Research what positive improvements were made to Kenya by Jomo Kenyatta.
3. Which do you think is a more effective means of gaining freedom: political strategy or guerrilla warfare? Explain your answer.

Cross-curricular Connections

Math: The entire border of Kenya is 3,446 km long, 3,308 km of that is shared with another country. What percentage of Kenya's border is not shared with another country?

Science: Kenya has gone through several major droughts. Research the cause and effects of drought in Africa.

South Africa and the System of Apartheid

For many years, Europeans were looking for a shorter way to get to Asia and the only way was to go around Africa. Since the tip of South Africa, now known as The Cape of Good Hope, was the last logical chance European sailors had to stop, rest and restock their supplies before reaching Asia, many Europeans docked there and established settlements where they conducted trade with the local Africans and other European groups.

In the beginning, the majority of Europeans that settled in South Africa were the Germans and the Dutch. The Dutch came to be called "Afrikaners", which is the Dutch name for Africans. Around 1800, the British took over the Dutch colony of South Africa and made English the official language and began forcing British culture on the African population.

At first, the two groups lived in relative peace, but as more Europeans came and wanted additional land, the different African ethnic groups were pushed off of their land. Soon the Afrikaners began to enslave the black Africans and forced them to work their newly acquired land. Black Africans fought back constantly, and an African named Shaka from the Zulu ethnic group united many of the African ethnic groups in the area. They fought the Europeans and moved some of them out.

In 1948, the Afrikaners passed a series of laws that came to be known as Apartheid. Apartheid means "apartness" in the Afrikaans language. Under the Apartheid system, black Africans had no rights, and were to be completely segregated from the white Afrikaner and British citizens. The system of Apartheid divided the people of South Africa into 4 groups: black African, Colored (mixed), Asian (Indian,

Chinese, etc), and white. Anyone that was not white had limited rights and was not allowed to go to school with, live with, work with, eat with, or interact with anyone who was white. Blacks were treated especially harsh, and were not allowed to own land, vote, and were made to carry a "pass book" everywhere they went. The pass book was for anyone not white and stated what race they were, where they lived, and where they worked. If you were caught without your pass you could be severely punished and even sent to jail.

Since the British and Afrikaners used force to put Apartheid in place, they faced a lot of resistance from the African population. Africans protested in the streets, fought the police, and formed political groups like the African National Congress (ANC) in resistance to the Apartheid system. One of the leaders in the fight against Apartheid was Nelson Mandela.

Nelson Mandela was a black South African, a lawyer, and the leader of the African National Congress (ANC). He fought constantly against the system of Apartheid through political resistance, nonviolent protest, and violent guerrilla warfare. In 1962 he was placed in jail for inciting riots, and was sentenced to life in prison. As Africans and the rest of the world fought to end Apartheid, they put pressure on the government to release Nelson Mandela. Finally, in 1990, after spending 27 years in prison, Nelson Mandela was freed and the system of Apartheid ended. In 1994, South Africa held its first democratic elections and Nelson Mandela was elected as South Africa's first black president and remained president until 1999. Sadly, Nelson Mandela died on December 5, 2013 from a respiratory infection. He was 95 years old.

Show What You Know! – South Africa and the System of Apartheid

Reading for Understanding

1. What caused Europeans to first start coming to South Africa?

   _____

   _____

   _____

2. Who were the Afrikaners and what did they do?

   _____

   _____

   _____

3. What did the system of Apartheid do?

   _____

   _____

   _____

4. What were the passbooks used for?

   _____

   _____

   _____

5. Who was Nelson Mandela and why was he important in South African history?

   _____

   _____

   _____

Take it to the Next Level

1. Research the Jim Crow system used in the United States and compare and contrast it to the system of Apartheid.
2. Research the life of Nelson Mandela and write a biographical report about him.
3. Many South Africans protested Apartheid by marching in the streets with signs. Create three different protest signs with images, symbols and messages that illustrate the feelings of the South African people toward Apartheid.

Cross-curricular Connections

Math: If there are about 16,000 nautical miles between England and India, if one were to travel around Africa, and the average ship in the 1800s went 6 miles an hour, how many days would it take a ship to get from England to India?

Science: South Africa is rich with many valuable minerals. Research which are the top three most valuable minerals found in South Africa.

African Americans
After Slavery
[1865 ACE - 1930 ACE]

"Up, you mighty race, accomplish what you will." - Marcus Garvey

The Era of Reconstruction

The years from 1865 to 1877 in the United States are known as the years of Reconstruction. It was supposed to be a time where the nation focused on rebuilding and reconstructing the country, specifically the south, after it had been destroyed by the Civil War. However, it was also a time that the country was supposed to focus on integrating formerly enslaved people into the country as full citizens with the same rights given to other members of society.

There were three major laws passed after the Civil War that were supposed to guarantee equal rights to recently freed black people. They were:

- The Thirteenth Amendment: Outlawed slavery of any kind for all people.
- The Fourteenth Amendment: States that African Americans were officially citizens of the United States.
- The Fifteenth Amendment: Guaranteed African American males the right to vote.

The passing of the 13th, 14th, and 15th Amendments might have guaranteed African American people certain rights under the law, however attaining those rights was not going to be so easy. Most African Americans emerging from slavery were illiterate, had few skills, could not write or do math, had never been off of their plantation, and did not understand how the government or the larger world around them worked. Freedom itself presented an entirely new set of problems for former slaves and they needed help from the government, the army, and charitable white organizations to help them make this transition from slavery to freedom.

The Freedman's Bureau was an organization created by the government right before the Civil War ended to aid the newly freed African Americans and to supply them with a variety of supports to ease their transition into a free society. It was also

ATLANTA BAPTIST SEMINARY.

responsible for using the army to help protect newly freed African Americans from angry whites who did not believe that they should be free. It was through the Freedman's Bureau that the idea of giving reparations to all former enslaved people by dividing up all of the former slave owners' land and giving each former slave 40 acres and a mule to work it came from. Predictably, congress later rejected the idea. The Freedman's Bureau also helped newly freed African Americans with finding food, jobs, homes, and education. The Freedman's Bureau was also responsible for the establishment of over 4000 schools throughout the south for the education of young African American children by 1870. The most famous of today's HBCUs like Howard, Spelman, Morehouse, Fisk, Hampton, and Tuskegee were all started as private colleges through the work of the Freedman's Bureau.

One of the biggest hurdles that newly freed African Americans had to get over was the issue of figuring out their identity. For generations, African Americans had been named by their slave owners and most of the time they were not even given a last name. So, when African Americans were freed, they had to choose last names for themselves. Many African Americans chose the last name of the former slave owner because they did not know anything different. Some blacks chose last names of famous whites of the time such as Washington (after George Washington), Lincoln (after Abraham Lincoln), Johnson (after Andrew Johnson), Jackson (after Andrew Jackson), and Lee (after Robert E. Lee), which would explain why many African Americans carry those last names today. Many of the freed slaves could not write, so some chose last names that suited either their status, job, or aspirations, such as Freedman, Blackman, or even White.

It was during Reconstruction that one finds the first African American elected politicians, and ironically, they came from the South. Hiram Revels and Blanche Bruce were the first two African American Senators and they were both from Mississippi. Eventually, there were over 20 African Americans elected to hold seats in the House of Representatives in several southern states. It was because of these early black politicians that laws were passed that truly benefited African Americans and helped them gain equality in the nation.

THE FIRST COLORED SENATOR AND REPRESENTATIVES,
In the 41st and 42nd Congress of the United States.

Reconstruction was a chance for the United States to make corrections for all of the crimes committed against black people during slavery, and in the beginning, it seemed like that was exactly what was going to happen. Unfortunately, what African Americans quickly discovered was that it would take a lot more than a few new laws, schools, and black politicians to change the racist mindset held by many white Americans that had been fostered during slavery.

Show What You Know! – The Era of Reconstruction

Reading for Understanding

1. What was the purpose of Reconstruction?

_____

_____

_____

2. What were the 13th, 14th, and 15th Amendments?

_____

_____

_____

3. What was the Freedman's Bureau and what did it accomplish?

_____

_____

_____

4. What were some of the ways that African Americans chose their last names once slavery was over?

_____

_____

_____

5. What political gains did African Americans make during Reconstruction?

_____

_____

_____

Take it to the Next Level

1. Research a particular HBCU that you are interested in, and create a poster or PowerPoint presentation that describes that school.
2. Research the history of your last name. Where does it come from? What does it mean? Share your findings with your family members.
3. The 15th Amendment gave the right to vote to all men, however women did not get the right to vote until the 19th Amendment. Research about the women's right to vote movement (known as the women's suffrage movement) and write a report about what you learned.

Cross-curricular Connections

Math: If the first enslaved people were brought to America in 1619 and slavery ended in 1865 with the passing of the 13th Amendment, then how many years did slavery exist in the United States?

Science: Research which HBCUs have the best programs for the following scientific fields: Pre-Med; Dental; Marine Biology; Engineering; Veterinary Sciences.

The End of Reconstruction

Rutherford B. Hayes

On April 14, 1865, Abraham Lincoln was assassinated while attending a performance at the Ford Theater by a man named John Wilkes Booth. Andrew Johnson became president after Lincoln died and it was under his administration that most of the Reconstruction reforms took place. However, by 1877, all of the revolting southern states had been readmitted back into the Union and the nation was looking for a way to heal the tension between the North and the South. It was at this time that Rutherford B. Hayes was elected president. During Hayes' presidency all of the work that was done during Reconstruction to help black Americans was undone and Reconstruction officially ended.

One of the first acts that Hayes put into motion was the removal of all Union troops out of the South. This was very significant to African Americans because the troops were helping enforce the laws that were enacted during Reconstruction like the 13th, 14th, and 15th Amendments. Without the troops, many states chose to ignore the new laws, leaving African Americans to fend for themselves.

Now that white people had control over state legislatures again (because all of the black people that had been elected during Reconstruction had been voted out), they began to pass laws in their states with the intention of overturning the laws that gave blacks equal rights to whites; these laws were called Black Codes and would later be known as Jim Crow laws. Many of the laws focused on reversing the 15th Amendment that guaranteed all citizens the right to vote. Some of the laws included imposing unfair restrictions specifically on black people, that included being able to read and write to be able to vote; or they had to own property; or they had to be able to recite the Constitution of the United States from memory. The most famous of the Jim Crow voting laws was called the Grandfather Clause. This Black Code stated that the only way a person could vote was if their grandfather voted. Since most of the grandfathers of African Americans living at that time had been enslaved, it essentially meant that no African American could vote.

White Americans used their recently regained political power to use the courts to strip away the rights of African Americans. The case of Plessy vs. Ferguson in 1896 was probably the most famous and most influential court case that was tried by the Supreme Court in the nation's history. It essentially reversed the 14th Amendment, which granted citizenship to African American people. The case involved a black man named Homer Plessy who was arrested for sitting in a seat on a train in Louisiana that was reserved for whites. Plessy believed that since he was a citizen, he should be allowed to sit wherever he wanted. The Supreme

Court disagreed with him and upheld the idea of segregated facilities for whites and blacks.

After slavery and Reconstruction, many African Americans struggled to start careers and gain new forms of employment. Most African Americans at this time were living in poverty and did not have enough money or resources to farm land of their own. This caused many African Americans to turn to southern white farmers for work in an arrangement known as sharecropping. Sharecropping was when an African American farmer entered into an agreement with a white landowner which stated that in exchange for being able to live on the land the black farmer had to work the land and at the harvest, he or she would give half of what was earned to the landowner as rent. In this system, the white owners often cheated the black farmers by saying they owed more than they did (remember, most blacks were not very educated at this time), or by making them purchase all of their tools, seeds, and other supplies from the land owner, which also plunged many black families into debt. It was often impossible for many African Americans to eliminate their debt because it increased faster than their ability to pay it off, which put them at the mercy of the white landowner.

Arguably, one of the worst things to happen to African Americans during the era of Reconstruction was the founding of the Ku Klux Klan. In 1866, in Tennessee, a group of former Confederate soldiers met to try and figure out what they could do to stop black people from progressing in society. They created a secret organization called the Ku Klux Klan for the sole purpose of terrorizing black people. The "Klan" as they were known, used violence, intimidation, kidnapping, rape, and murder to put fear into African American communities throughout the south. With the withdrawal of Union troops in 1877, there was no one left to protect the lives and property of African people from the threat of the Klan.

Many African Americans hoped that the end of the Civil War and the changes made during Reconstruction would finally result in them leading peaceful, productive lives. Much to their dismay, a large number of white Americans were not ready or willing to allow black people an equal place in society, and as was seen in the years after Reconstruction, were prepared to do anything in their power to prevent that from happening.

Show What You Know! – The End of Reconstruction

Reading for Understanding

1. What effect did Hayes' removal of federal troops from the south have on African Americans?

   _____

   _____

   _____

2. What tactics were used to try and keep African Americans from voting?

   _____

   _____

   _____

3. Describe the Plessy vs. Ferguson case and why it was important.

   _____

   _____

   _____

4. What was sharecropping? Why was it harmful to African Americans?

   _____

   _____

   _____

5. Why was the Ku Klux Klan created?

   _____

   _____

   _____

Take it to the Next Level

1. Imagine you are an African American living in the south; write a letter to a friend or relative living in the north describing what's happening now that Hayes is president.
2. Write a rap or a song about what happened during Reconstruction.
3. Research the growth and rise of the Ku Klux Klan and write a report about what you learned.

Cross-curricular Connections

Math: Mr. Mitchell and his family are sharecroppers on Mr. Lee's cotton farm. They get paid $.33 for every pound of cotton they pick. However, they also have to rent tools from Mr. Lee at $21.00 per month as well as other supplies that cost $11.50 per month. How many pounds of cotton would the Mitchell family need to pick in order for them not to owe Mr. Lee money at the end of the month?

Science: Out of the following crops, which was the most profitable and easiest to grow: cotton, tobacco, rice, or corn?

Booker T. Washington

At the beginning of the 20th century, tensions were still high between white and black Americans, but it was becoming clear that they would have to find a way to coexist in society. Most whites at the time felt that black people were inferior and should not enjoy the same rights as white people. Conversely, black people felt like they should enjoy all of the same rights, privileges and opportunities as their white counterparts. However, not everyone agreed on the methods that black people should use to establish themselves into the American mainstream. The three black men who led the country in trying to figure out what blacks' role should be in American society were Booker T. Washington, W.E.B. Du Bois, and Marcus Garvey.

Booker T. Washington was born into slavery in Virginia around 1856. His mother was a cook on the plantation on which they lived, and his father was an unknown white man, possibly from a nearby plantation. He was nine years old when slavery was abolished. He first became interested in education as a young boy when he would sit outside the window of the school house on the plantation and watched as all the young white children learned how to read and write. As a young man he worked in the coal mines of West Virginia until around the age of sixteen, when he enrolled in the Hampton Institute (later known as Hampton University). At Hampton, he was a good student and was known to be an excellent public speaker. When he graduated from Hampton in 1876, Washington returned to West Virginia to become a teacher. Soon after that, he returned to Hampton as a professor. In 1881, at the age of 25, Washington opened an all-black school in Alabama called the Tuskegee Institute, later to be known as Tuskegee University.

At Tuskegee, Washington offered courses in agriculture, dairy farming, carpentry, and other manual labor skills. He did not offer courses in English, math, history, or general sciences which aligned

with his beliefs of how black people should gain power in the United States. He believed that African Americans should not seek political power or pursue the same type of education offered at white colleges. Instead, he felt what was most beneficial for the black community was to pursue a future as skilled craftsmen and manual laborers and not try to gain power through politics but instead through economics. In a speech he gave in 1895 at the Atlanta Cotton States Exposition, he went even further when he stated that blacks and whites should stay segregated except for when blacks were working for whites. This speech, which became known as the "Atlanta Compromise," gained Washington a lot of support from whites but angered many in the black community who felt that he was not trying to gain equal rights for blacks.

Washington's belief that black people should pull themselves up by their own bootstraps, and gain the skills necessary to improve their own communities without assistance from white people made him very well known. While not everyone agreed with his philosophies, Booker T. Washington provided African Americans opportunities for advancement at a time when black people were still trying to secure a foothold in a post slavery society.

Show What You Know! – Booker T. Washington

Reading for Understanding

1. Describe three aspects of Washington's childhood.

   _____

   _____

   _____

2. What was the name of the school that Washington started? What subjects were taught there?

   _____

   _____

   _____

3. What methods did Washington think African Americans should use to gain power in the United States?

   _____

   _____

   _____

4. What did Washington express in his "Atlanta Compromise" speech?

   _____

   _____

   _____

5. Do you agree with Washington's ideas in his "Atlanta Compromise" speech? Why or why not?

   _____

   _____

   _____

Take it to the Next Level

1. Hampton University and Tuskegee University are both HBCUs. Research the various requirements necessary in order to gain admittance into each school.
2. Washington's autobiography was entitled, *Up From Slavery*. Read Washington's autobiography and write a book report about it.
3. Read the next section on W.E.B. Du Bois and compare and contrast the beliefs of the two leaders using a chart or illustrations.

Cross Curricular Connections

Math: Washington walked 500 miles from his home in order to enroll in the Hampton Institute. The average person walks about 3 miles per hour. If Washington walked for 10 hours a day at an average speed of 3 miles per hour, how long would it take him to walk 500 miles to Hampton Institute?

Science: George Washington Carver was a professor at Tuskegee Institute and taught agricultural science. Research the different accomplishments and inventions of George Washington Carver, and how they have impacted our world today.

W.E.B. Du Bois

William Edward Burghardt Du Bois was born in Massachusetts in 1868 and grew up in a mostly white town where he interacted with whites on a daily basis. He possessed an above average intelligence, and attended Fisk University in Nashville, Tennessee, and then Harvard University where he became the first African American to earn a Ph.D.

Du Bois is considered one of the most brilliant men in history and wrote 21 books, and hundreds of published essays. His most famous book is *The Souls of Black Folk* which he wrote in 1903. In this

book he explores and describes the experiences of black people in America and introduced readers to the notion that black people live constantly with a "double-consciousness." He describes this as a constant battle that African Americans go through as they try to blend in with the standards and culture of American society, while also trying to hold on to and value their own black culture and identity. In the book he states, "one ever feels his twoness - an American, a Negro; two souls, two thoughts, two unreconciled strivings; two warring ideals in one dark body, whose dogged strength alone keeps it from being torn asunder."

Du Bois was also one of the co-founders of the National Association for the Advancement of Colored People (NAACP) which he helped create in 1909 as an agency to help fight legal segregation.

Through the NAACP, Du Bois also created its monthly magazine *The Crisis*, which covered the many different aspects of African American life and culture.

His views were almost completely opposite to several other black scholars of his time such as Booker T. Washington. Du Bois believed that blacks should not settle for being second class citizens but should strive for equality. He believed in fighting for equal rights both socially and politically, and that blacks should be educated in all areas, especially history. Du Bois felt that African Americans would never gain full inclusion in American society if they did not exercise the right to vote and did not strive to get as liberal an education as possible.

In the latter years of his life, Dr. Du Bois left the United States and moved to Ghana where he studied and practiced Pan-Africanism, which is the philosophy that states that people of African descent around the globe should unite and work toward their collective improvement. He died in Ghana in 1963 at the age of 95. Throughout his life, at a time when African Americans were denied opportunities at every turn, W.E.B. Du Bois was able to accomplish things that many thought were impossible for African Americans and his work continues to be an inspiration to many in the black community today.

Show What you Know! – W.E.B. Du Bois

Reading for Understanding

1. What academic accomplishments did W.E.B. Du Bois achieve?

    _____

    _____

    _____

2. In your own words describe Du Bois' theory of "double-consciousness."

    _____

    _____

    _____

3. What was the purpose of the NAACP?

    _____

    _____

    _____

4. What methods did Du Bois suggest African Americans should use to gain equal status in American society?

    _____

    _____

    _____

5. When Du Bois became older, to where did he relocate, and what did he do while there?

    _____

    _____

    _____

Take it to the Next Level

1. Research the two main schools that Du Bois attended, Fisk and Harvard, and determine the various requirements to gain admittance to each school.
2. Create a chart with African on one side and American on the other side and list all of the aspects of American culture practiced by African Americans under the American side. Then list all of the aspects of African culture practiced by African Americans on the African side.
3. Do you agree with Du Bois' belief that African Americans need to be able to vote in order to gain equality and power in the United States? Explain your answer in a paragraph.

Cross Curricular Connections

Math: When Du Bois enrolled at Fisk University in 1885 it cost about $100 a year to attend. In 2019 it costs $32,705. What is the percent increase of tuition from 1885 to 2019?

Science: As the theory of "double-consciousness" pertains to African Americans, some have compared it to a type of schizophrenia. Research the causes and symptoms of schizophrenia and write a response explaining whether you agree with that idea or not.

Marcus Garvey

Marcus Garvey, the father of the "back to Africa" movement, was born in St. Ann's Bay, Jamaica in 1887. He was the last of eleven children and did not have much of a formal education, instead he taught himself how to read from his father's extensive library. He quit school at the age of 14 to work for a newspaper as a printer's apprentice which allowed him to travel all over the Caribbean. In that role, he noticed that the lives of black people in all of the colonies he visited were terrible and were being made so at the hands of the Europeans that controlled them. He decided that he needed to be able to speak out about what he saw, so he enrolled at a university in London, England to work on his speaking and debating skills.

After returning to Jamaica in 1912, he founded the Universal Negro Improvement Association (UNIA) with the goal of uniting people in the African diaspora and to "establish a country and absolute government of their own." He used the UNIA to teach black people about their history and make them proud to be black. He also thought that black people should create their own businesses and not depend on white people to get all that they needed to survive. Because of this belief, Garvey used the UNIA to set up businesses throughout many black communities. The main offices of UNIA were located in Harlem, New York; it was there that he helped establish black laundromats, black newspapers, black nurses, black restaurants, black grocery stores, and even a black army.

Marcus Garvey believed heavily in the philosophy of Pan-Africanism, which is the belief that

people of African descent throughout the diaspora should join together to fight against their common oppressor, and improve their political, economic, and social well-being. To help bring his vision of an economically thriving global African community to reality, Garvey created the Black Star Line, a shipping company that would be used to trade goods between black people throughout the world. In addition, the Black Star Line was also to be used to transport black people back to Africa in an attempt to establish a new black nation in the current country of Liberia. Unfortunately, due to problems with the ships and their crews, none of the ships Garvey purchased ever made it to Africa.

Garvey's plans to unite black people in the diaspora caught the attention of the new head of the Bureau of Investigation (later known as the F.B.I.), J. Edgar Hoover. Hoover did everything he could to undermine the efforts of Garvey, which included trying to find damaging personal information about him, and even hiring the first black F.B.I. agent, who was sent into the UNIA as a spy and even helped sabotage the engines of the ships in the Black Star Line.

In 1922, Garvey and three other UNIA employees were charged with mail fraud for selling stock in a ship to UNIA members that had not yet been purchased. Garvey was sentenced to five years imprisonment in Atlanta, Georgia; however, he was released in 1927 and deported to Jamaica. Upon his arrival in Jamaica, he continued his work with the UNIA, but it had lost a lot of its momentum and support while he was in jail. In a final attempt to reignite his organization, he moved to London, England, but he could not revive it. In 1940, after suffering several strokes, Garvey passed away. He taught black pride and self-determination that led to the largest global black movement in history and cemented him as being remembered as one of the greatest black civil rights leaders of all time.

Show What You Know! – Marcus Garvey

Reading for Understanding

1. What drove Marcus Garvey to go back to school and improve his speaking skills?

   _____

   _____

   _____

2. What was the name and goal of the organization that Garvey created?

   _____

   _____

   _____

3. What is Pan-Africanism?

   _____

   _____

   _____

4. What was the purpose of the Black Star Line and was it successful?

   _____

   _____

   _____

5. What caused Marcus Garvey's movement to fail?

   _____

   _____

   _____

Take it to the Next Level

1. Write a rap or poem that describes what Marcus Garvey wanted to accomplish.
2. Create a map or mural of a fictional town where all of the businesses, public services, and institutions are owned and controlled by black people.
3. Create a fictional talk show where two people are arguing whether they should join Marcus Garvey and try to go back to Africa.

Cross-curricular Connections

Math: Conduct a survey of your community. How many black owned businesses are located in your neighborhood? How many non-black owned businesses exist in your community?

Science: Marcus Garvey died of complications due to several strokes. Research what causes people to suffer from strokes and how it impacts their bodies.

The Harlem Renaissance

The Harlem Renaissance refers to the period of time between the early 1900s and 1930 during which there was an explosion of African American art, music and literature coming out of Harlem, New York. While Harlem was the center of this cultural movement, it was not the only place that a renaissance occurred. Other major cities in the United States, such as Chicago, Cleveland and Los Angeles, were also experiencing their own similar cultural resurgence.

Harlem is a neighborhood in the northern part of Manhattan in New York City. It was originally a neighborhood created for rich whites in the late 1800s, however due to the overproduction of apartment and office spaces, landlords looked to blacks to fill their vacant buildings. African Americans were already moving in large numbers to the north as a result of the Great Migration, which was the movement of African Americans out of the south and to the northern and western states in search of jobs and better opportunities. So, as they reached New York, many of these migrating blacks gravitated toward Harlem, soon making it the unofficial capital of black wealth, culture and excellence in the United States.

At the start of the Harlem Renaissance, slavery had only been over for 40 years and the opinion held by many white Americans was that African Americans were inferior and were not capable of contributing to society in any meaningful way. The accomplishments made by many African Americans during the Harlem Renaissance created the idea of a "New Negro" that defied the stereotypes believed by many white people and sought to create an image that served as a source of upliftment, pride and inspiration for the black community. During the Harlem Renaissance, African Americans thrived. They were creating and running their own businesses, attaining new levels of education, writing books, newspaper articles, poems, as well as transforming multiple genres of music and dance.

Some of the most famous individuals from African American history got their start during the Harlem Renaissance. Alain Locke is widely considered to be the chief architect behind the Harlem Renaissance. He encouraged artists and writers to look toward Africa as a source of inspiration and pride, and to focus their work on the black experience to help fight against negative stereotypes about African American people. Writers like Langston Hughes, Zora Neale Hurston, and Countee Cullen expressed in words the feelings, hopes and experiences of the black American that had previously been unpublished. Legendary musicians and performers such as Duke Ellington, Billie Holiday, Paul Robeson, Cab Calloway, Josephine Baker, Louis Armstrong, and Count Basie entertained both black and white crowds in venues like the Cotton Club with their unique and innovative styles of music. W.E.B. DuBois, Marcus Garvey and Walter White led the charge in black intellectual activism by trying to inspire blacks to rise up and improve their lives and communities through education and self-pride.

The end of the Harlem Renaissance coincides with the stock market crash of 1929 that sent the country spiraling into the Great Depression. African Americans were hit especially hard by the depression, and with jobs and affordable housing growing scarce, African Americans did not have the resources to produce or consume many of the art, music and writing that they had been used to. In addition, many of the most talented African Americans left Harlem in search for other opportunities, causing Harlem to fall deeper into poverty. Despite its abrupt end, the Harlem Renaissance had a tremendous impact on African American culture both then and for many years to come. It paved the way for the success of many modern authors, poets and musicians and its focus on black pride and equality laid the foundations for the Civil Rights Movement.

Show What You Know! – The Harlem Renaissance

Reading for Understanding
1. What was the Harlem Renaissance?

_____

_____

_____

2. What caused African Americans to move to Harlem?

_____

_____

_____

3. How did the Harlem Renaissance go against the stereotypes held by many white Americans?

_____

_____

_____

4. Who were some of the most significant individuals who had their start during the Harlem Renaissance?

_____

_____

_____

5. What caused the decline of the Harlem Renaissance?

_____

_____

_____

Take it to the Next Level
1. One of Langston Hughes' most famous poems is "A Dream Deferred". Read this poem and apply it to the experience of African American people in the United States.
2. Watch videos of Josephine Baker and Paul Robeson online. Which modern artists would you compare them to and why?
3. Research what it was like in the Cotton Club and then draw a picture illustrating a scene from a typical night.

Cross-curricular Connections
Math: In 1910, the black population of Harlem was 181,949. In 1920, the black population of Harlem was 216,026. By what percent did the population of Harlem increase from 1910 to 1920?
Science: Many of our everyday household items were invented by African Americans during the Harlem Renaissance. Research who some of the leading inventors of that time were and what they created.

The Civil Rights Movement

[1954 ACE - 1969 ACE]

"We declare our right on this earth to be a man, to be a human being, to be respected as a human being, to be given the rights of a human being in this society, on this earth, in this day, which we intend to bring into existence by any means necessary." - Malcolm X

The Civil Rights Movement

The struggle to end social injustice, discrimination, and gain equal rights for African Americans during the 1950s and 1960s is commonly known as the Civil Rights Movement.

Legal segregation and discrimination existed in the United States during slavery, and into the period known as Reconstruction with the passing of the "Jim Crow" laws. These laws that established separate schools, toilets, water fountains, and outlawed certain practices like interracial marriages, and blacks living in neighborhoods with whites, were found mostly in the south however northern blacks also faced discrimination when trying to find a job, buy a home, or gain an education.

Jim Crow laws became solidified in 1896 when the Supreme Court passed its judgement in the landmark case of *Plessy vs Ferguson*. Homer Plessy was a black man who was riding on a train in 1892 traveling from New Orleans, Louisiana to Covington, Louisiana. He was sitting in the white only section

and refused to sit in the section reserved for blacks. He was subsequently arrested and proceeded to fight his case in court on the basis that segregated facilities violated his 14th Amendment rights as a citizen of the United States. The case made it all the way to the Supreme Court who ruled that segregated facilities are indeed constitutional, as long as they are "separate but equal". They further ruled that the 14th Amendment only applied to political and civil rights, not social rights, like how someone chooses to travel. As a result, passenger trains were the first to become completely legally segregated, but it soon spread to buses, swimming pools, hotels, theaters, and schools.

African Americans continued to challenge these unjust laws in a variety of ways, which eventually lead to the Supreme Court ruling that segregated public accommodations were unconstitutional in the landmark case of *Brown vs Board of Education* in 1954. However, many parts of the south, still steeped in the racist tradition of Jim Crow refused to change, and openly ignored the court's decision.

It wasn't until 1955 when a 42-year-old woman working as a secretary for the Montgomery chapter of the NAACP named Rosa Parks refused to give up her seat in the white section of the bus to a white man did the Civil Rights movement begin to take off. While Parks was not the first person to ever refuse to give up their seat to a white person, this action, which had been planned by Parks and the NAACP ahead of time, sparked the Montgomery bus boycott and introduced the nation to a young preacher by the name of Martin Luther King, Jr. Over the next two decades, a multitude of groups and individuals, both black and white, fought and struggled to gain equal political, economic, educational, and

social rights for African Americans they believed were guaranteed to them by birth as American citizens.

Show What You Know! – The Civil Rights Movement

Reading for Understanding

1. What were Jim Crow laws?

_____

_____

_____

2. Why did Homer Plessy think that segregated trains violated his 14th Amendment rights?

_____

_____

_____

3. How did the Supreme Court respond to Plessy's claim?

_____

_____

_____

4. What did the *Brown vs. Board of Education* case do?

_____

_____

_____

5. What impact did Rosa Parks' actions have on the country?

_____

_____

_____

Take it to the Next Level

1. Research the Civil Rights Movement and create a timeline that illustrates the 10 most important events from that time period.
2. Create a list of 10 actual Jim Crow laws enacted by some of the southern states.
3. Draw the scene where Rosa Parks refused to give up her seat to a white man on the bus.

Cross Curricular Connections

Math: If the distance from New Orleans to Covington, Louisiana is 42 miles and the train in which Homer Plessy was riding was traveling at a rate of 22 miles/hour and made 2 stops that lasted 7 minutes each, how long did it take Mr. Plessy to reach Covington?

Science: Many of the Jim Crow laws were enacted under the assumption that black and white people were not equal because they look different from each other. Research the genetic characteristics that cause the physical differences between different races.

Martin Luther King, Jr.

Martin Luther King, Jr. was born in Atlanta, Georgia on January 15, 1929. His father was a pastor, and his mother was a former school teacher. They, along with his brother and sister, grew up in Atlanta's Sweet Auburn neighborhood, one of the most prosperous African American neighborhoods in the country.

As a child, Martin was a very gifted student and excelled in his school work. At the young age of 15, Martin was admitted into Morehouse College where he aspired to study medicine and law. It was only after being mentored by the college's president and a well-known theologian, Benjamin Elijah Mays, that he decided to follow in his father's footsteps and become a minister.

After graduating from Morehouse in 1948, King enrolled in Crozer Theological Seminary in Pennsylvania where he received his bachelor's degree in divinity. King continued his religious studies at Boston University where he earned his doctorate in divinity in 1953. While in Boston, he met a young singer named Coretta Scott who was studying music. The two fell in love and were married in 1953. After graduating from Boston University, King received an appointment to pastor Dexter Avenue Baptist Church in Montgomery, Alabama. The couple moved to Montgomery where they had four children: Yolanda, Martin Luther King III, Dexter, and Bernice.

Martin Luther King, Jr. was thrust onto the public stage when Rosa Parks refused to give up her seat on a bus to a white man in Montgomery, Alabama on December 1, 1955. This act of defiance was the spark that started the Montgomery Bus Boycott, a movement that was spearheaded by Dr. King. He employed the strategies of nonviolent resistance and noncooperation that he learned from the Indian freedom fighter Mohandas Gandhi, black activist Bayard Rustin, and white organizer Miles Horton. The black, mostly female, residents of Montgomery refused to ride the public bus system in opposition of its racist, segregationist practices. Instead of riding the bus they carpooled or walked for a total of 381 days, effectively shutting down the Montgomery public transit system and forcing the city to change its policy on designated seating for black and white customers.

The Bus Boycott made Dr. King a national symbol for nonviolence and the fight for African Americans' civil rights. Unfortunately, his new found celebrity status also made him a target of the FBI. In 1955, the FBI began monitoring Dr. King's movements and phone calls through their domestic counterintelligence program called COINTELPRO. Through this program, the FBI gathered information on Dr. King with the aim of discrediting him and his movement.

In 1957, Dr. King, along with several other prominent ministers and civil rights activists, formed the Southern Christian Leadership Conference (SCLC), an organization dedicated to using nonviolent activism to achieve equal rights for black people. King was elected as the SCLC's president and used the position to further speak out against the injustices facing African Americans across the country.

In 1960, Dr. King moved with his family back to Atlanta where he co-pastored Ebenezer Baptist Church with his father Martin Luther King, Sr. He continued to be involved in the fight against segregation and racist practices using nonviolent techniques. Despite his stance on nonviolence, Dr. King was beaten, cursed at, spit on, and arrested multiple times. Throughout it all he never gave up on his belief that nonviolent activism was the best tactic to be used in order to gain equal rights for African Americans.

One of King's greatest accomplishments was his involvement in the planning of the March on Washington for Jobs and Freedom. The event took place on August 28, 1963 in front of the Lincoln Memorial in Washington DC and drew in between two hundred and three hundred thousand people of all races. It was advertised as a peaceful rally to protest the country's racial injustices. It was at this rally that Dr. King gave his famous speech, "I Have a Dream." His work in nonviolence and racial justice also allowed for Dr. King to be awarded the Nobel Peace Prize; he was the youngest person to ever receive the award.

Voting rights for African Americans was a major issue that Dr. King fought for. At that time in the south, African Americans were denied the right to vote using a variety of racist tactics including expensive poll taxes, literacy tests, and policies such as the "Grandfather Clause", which stated that if your grandfather couldn't vote then you couldn't vote either. Since the grandfathers of the majority of African Americans in the south at this time had been slaves, it essentially disenfranchised, or took away the right to vote, from almost all African Americans. Dr. King worked extensively with the Student Nonviolent Coordinating Committee (SNCC) to register African American voters as well as protest the unfair policies used in many states to keep African Americans from voting. Dr. King also worked closely with President Lyndon Johnson to secure voting rights for black people, which led to the passing of the Voting Rights Act of 1965 that guaranteed African Americans the right to vote.

Dr. King began to shift his focus from civil rights for African Americans to larger societal issues affecting all Americans such as poverty and the Vietnam War. King's stance was that war and poverty were forms of violence and that violence anywhere against anyone was completely unacceptable. In 1967, he launched his Poor People's Campaign which was to gain economic justice for poor people in the United States.

In April of 1968, Dr. King traveled to Memphis, Tennessee to support a group of sanitation workers who were on strike in order to receive better pay. While standing on the balcony of his hotel, Dr. King was shot and killed by a man named James Earl Ray. Dr. King will forever be remembered as not only the leader of the Civil Rights Movement, but also as a man who dedicated his life to a belief that all people are created equal and should be treated that way, and, as he stated in his "I Have a Dream" speech, "...live in a nation where they will not be judged by the color of their skin but by the content of their character."

Show What You Know! – Martin Luther King, Jr.

Reading for Understanding

1. What kind of impact do you think Dr. King's education had on his life and decision to join the Civil Rights Movement?

   _____
   _____
   _____

2. What did the citizens of Montgomery do to change the policy of the Montgomery bus system?

   _____
   _____
   _____

3. What was the purpose of the SCLC?

   _____
   _____
   _____

4. What did Dr. King do to address the voting rights issues that were facing many African Americans?

   _____
   _____
   _____

5. Why do you think Dr. King shifted his focus to issues like poverty and the Vietnam war?

   _____
   _____
   _____

Take it to the Next Level

1. Create a comic book that illustrates Dr. King's life. Include pictures, dialogue, and captions that explain the different scenes.
2. Memorize Dr. King's *I Have a Dream* speech and recite it in front of your family, friends or classmates.
3. Imagine that you are a talk show host and you have the opportunity to interview Dr. King. What do you think he would say about the state of African Americans today? What solutions do you think he would present to fix some of the issues we are dealing with as a society?

Cross-curricular Connections
Math: It is estimated that The Montgomery Bus Boycott cost the bus company $3,000 a day. If the boycott lasted 381 days, what was the total amount of money that the bus company lost?
Science: Research what the Medical Examiner's autopsy report said about how Dr. King died.

Ella Baker

There have been few women who have had a greater impact on the Civil Rights Movement in the United States than Ella Baker. Born in 1903 in Norfolk, Virginia, Ms. Baker was exposed very early to the idea of fighting against injustice when she used to listen to stories from her grandmother about her time as a slave. Her grandmother would explain to her how she fought for her own humanity when she refused to marry the person her former owner wanted her to. Ms. Baker loved her grandmother and was heavily influenced by her commitment to stand her ground and fight for what she believed was right.

As a student growing up in rural North Carolina, Ms. Baker was not your average student. She excelled at school and was accepted into the competitive Shaw University in Raleigh, North Carolina. After graduating from Shaw in 1927 as the valedictorian, she moved to New York City to begin her career in social activism. She quickly joined a group called the Young Negroes Cooperative League whose goal was to empower black people economically by collectively combining their resources; within a short time, she became the group's national director.

Around 1940 she joined the National Association for the Advancement of Colored People (NAACP), and as a field secretary she traveled around the country recruiting new members and raising funds for the organization. Her exemplary work with the NAACP allowed her to move up in the ranks quickly. In 1943, she became the National Director of branches and then in 1952 she became director of the entire New York Chapter of the NAACP.

In 1955, when Martin Luther King, Jr. started the Montgomery Bus Boycott, Ms. Baker was extremely inspired by both his leadership and his message. When Dr. King started the Southern Christian Leadership Conference (SCLC) in 1957, Ms. Baker was one of the first people to sign up to help him launch this new organization and served as the executive director of the Atlanta branch. Not afraid to speak her mind, Ms. Baker quickly gained a reputation for being a strong-willed woman who was not afraid to push back against the mostly male leadership of the SCLC when she did not agree with them.

In 1960, black students from North Carolina A&T University staged a nonviolent sit-in at a segregated Woolworth's lunch counter in Greensboro, North Carolina. After being denied service, they were met with savage beatings and verbal abuse. Ms. Baker heard about this event and knew she had to get involved. She left the SCLC and organized a meeting with the leaders of the Greensboro sit-ins. They discussed goals, strategy, and what kind of impact they wanted to have, and as a result of this meeting the Student Nonviolent Coordinating Committee (SNCC) was born. The group was responsible for a massive voter registration campaign for blacks in the south, and for conducting the Freedom Rides which challenged segregation at bus stations throughout the south. Ms. Baker also helped them form the Mississippi Freedom Democratic Party in 1964 which served as an alternative to the Democratic Party in Mississippi, which they felt was not meeting the needs of its black citizens.

Ms. Baker's role and impact on the Civil Rights Movement is often overlooked because she did not crave the limelight and did most of her work behind the scenes. But it cannot be mentioned enough that without her skill as an organizer and unwavering dedication to freedom, the Civil Rights Movement would not have turned out the way it did. Her leadership and influence on the young people of SNCC earned her the nickname Fundi, which is a Swahili word that means "a person who passes down a craft to the next generation", a name that aptly describes Ms. Baker's service to the Civil Rights Movement.

Show What You Know! – Ella Baker

Reading for Understanding

1. Where did Ella Baker learn about fighting for social justice?

   _____

   _____

   _____

2. What role did Ms. Baker have on the NAACP and the SCLC?

   _____

   _____

   _____

3. How was Ms. Baker viewed by many of the men of the SCLC?

   _____

   _____

   _____

4. What caused Ms. Baker to help form the Student Nonviolent Coordinating Committee?

   _____

   _____

   _____

5. Do you think the nickname Ms. Baker received fits who she was and what she did? Explain your answer.

   _____

   _____

   _____

Take it to the Next Level

1. Imagine you are Ella Baker applying for a job. Create a resume for her that outlines and illustrates her background, work experience, and accomplishments.
2. In your opinion, what event or decision had the largest impact on Ms. Baker's life? Explain your opinion.
3. Create an acrostic poem about Ella Baker's life and accomplishments using the letters in her name ELLA BAKER. An acrostic poem is a poem about a particular topic where each letter in the topic is used to start a sentence that relates to that topic.

Cross-curricular Connections

Math: Ms. Baker helped organize and plan the routes that would be taken by the Freedom Riders. If the bus route taken by the Freedom Riders from Washington, D.C. to New Orleans was 1,000 miles long and took 17 hours to complete, how many miles an hour did they travel?

Science: Research the different medical injuries that were sustained by some of the Freedom Riders.

Malcolm X

Malcolm X was born as Malcolm Little on May 19, 1925 in Omaha, Nebraska. His mother's name was Louise Little and his father's name was Earl Little; Malcolm had a total of seven brothers and sisters.

Earl Little was a Baptist preacher and a follower of Marcus Garvey, who believed that black people should control the businesses and institutions in their communities and should separate from white people in America and start their own nation in Africa. This caused problems for his family everywhere they went, because the white people in the towns they lived in did not like it when Earl Little tried to educate the blacks and unify them. After years of harassment from the Ku Klux Klan, and other white organizations, Earl Little's body was found dead after having been run over by a train. The police ruled that it was an accident but many people felt that he was murdered by the Ku Klux Klan.

After Malcolm's father died, the family fell on hard times. Louise Little had a hard time finding work because of her dead husband's reputation, causing the family to rapidly plunge into poverty. The kids became hard to manage, and Malcolm began stealing food and other things in his spare time. The state child services organization then split the family up and sent Malcolm to a foster home. Soon after, Malcolm's mother was admitted into a mental hospital after suffering a nervous breakdown.

Malcolm spent several years in the foster home and did very well in school and aspired to be a lawyer, until one day he was told by his teacher that being a lawyer was "no realistic goal for a nigger." Not long after that he lost interest in school and dropped out. He moved around to different cities such as Detroit and Boston and worked odd jobs like serving food on trains and shining shoes. He soon became involved in the criminal world; he sold and did drugs, ran numbers (the illegal lottery system conducted in many urban communities during the time), and committed robberies. During this time, he was known as Detroit Red, because of his red hair. Eventually he was caught burglarizing houses in Boston, Massachusetts with his best friend Shorty and two white women, he was sentenced to 10 years in prison.

It was during prison that Malcolm was first introduced to the religion of Islam by his brother Reginald. Reginald was a member of a type of Islam called the Nation of Islam (N.O.I.) which was ran by a man named Elijah Muhammad. Elijah Muhammad believed that he was the last of the prophets and that God, who, according to Elijah Muhammad, was black, sent him to free his people by teaching them their "true" religion, which was Islam. The Nation of Islam quickly gained a lot of followers due to their message of black upliftment and pride. In addition, they developed programs that helped many black people off of drugs and alcohol. However, what they became most known for was standing up to white people, and as Malcolm once put it, "telling the white man the truth to his face."

Mr. Muhammad taught black nationalism which meant that all of the stores, schools, and businesses in the black community should be controlled and ran by black people. Elijah Muhammad also believed that black people will never succeed as long as they are around white people and that they should separate from them completely and start their own country with their own land. Most controversially however was Elijah Muhammad's belief that white people were the "devil" and were completely evil.

It was in jail that he converted to the Nation of Islam and became a follower of Elijah Muhammad. He then changed his name from Malcolm Little to Malcolm X. People in the Nation of Islam often replace their last name with "X" because they know that the last names of black people in America belonged to the slave masters who owned their ancestors and was passed on to the slaves. The letter X in mathematics represent the unknown, because the true last names of black people in America are unknown because they were stolen from Africa and their heritage was not preserved.

When Malcolm X was released from prison, he became one of the Nation of Islam's best ministers and traveled the country teaching black people the truth about their history and encouraging them to start standing up to white people and fight for their equality. He greatly disagreed with the idea of nonviolence which was being made popular at the time by people like Martin Luther King, Jr. He did not believe in acting violently; however, he did believe in defending oneself against violence.

As the years went by, Malcolm found out that Elijah Muhammad had been having an affair with several young women in the Nation of Islam, and even had children with some of them. This crushed Malcolm, because he believed that Elijah Muhammad was the prophet of Allah (God) and was perfect. Soon after that, President John F. Kennedy was killed, and Malcolm made statements about the incident that Elijah Muhammad had forbid him from making, and Elijah silenced him for 90 days, during which time he was not to make any speeches or public statements of any kind. This began the period of turbulence between Malcolm and the Nation of Islam.

One of the duties that every Muslim has to fulfill at least once in their life time is a pilgrimage (trip) to the holy city of Mecca called a hajj. While Malcolm was having problems with the N.O.I. he decided to make that hajj. In Mecca, he experienced many things that changed his way of thinking. While he was there, he noticed unity between all Muslims, regardless of where they were from and what their skin color was. For him, this challenged the ideas of separation that he had been preaching while he was in the N.O.I. He began to see the religion of Islam as the cure for the racial ills that plagued the United States. Once a Muslim makes the hajj to Mecca then they can add to their name El-hajj, so Malcolm took the Muslim name El-hajj Malik El-Shabazz, which he used in the Muslim community, however for public events he continued to use the name Malcolm X.

When Malcolm came back to the United States he separated from the Nation of Islam and started his own organization called the Organization for Afro-American Unity (OAAU). His group's mission was to unify black people in the United States with black people in other countries, in an effort to fight for human rights for blacks all around the world. This pan-Africanist philosophy was quickly noticed by the FBI and the federal government and they began tapping Malcolm's phone and house. Malcolm began receiving death threats and he knew that the end of his life was near. Malcolm was killed on February 21, 1965 while giving a speech in New York by three gunmen who shot him 15 times. The three gunmen were members of the Nation of Islam, however many men believed that the men may have also worked for the FBI as spies.

Malcolm fought and died for the freedom of his people. He sought to liberate African Americans, and other black people throughout the diaspora, from the stranglehold of racism, discrimination, and oppression. Many consider him a controversial figure; however, no one can deny the fact that he was a source of inspiration and pride for millions of African Americans during the Civil Rights era, and continues to inspire black people today.

Show What You Know! – Malcolm X

Reading for Understanding

1. What impact do you think Malcolm's upbringing had on his later life?

   _____

   _____

   _____

2. Describe the views of Elijah Muhammad.

   _____

   _____

   _____

3. What is black nationalism?

   _____

   _____

   _____

4. What caused Malcolm to want to leave the Nation of Islam?

   _____

   _____

   _____

5. What was the purpose and goals of the Organization of Afro-American Unity?

   _____

   _____

   _____

Take it to the Next Level

1. Listen to Malcolm's speech entitled, "The Ballot or the Bullet" and describe what you think the main message was and how it can be applied today.
2. Malcolm X was known by many names throughout his life that represented different stages of his development: Malcolm Little, Detroit Red, Malcolm X, and El-hajj El Malik El Shabazz. Write an essay that describes how each of his names represents a different stage of his life.
3. Pretend you are a talk show host and your two guests are Malcolm X and Martin Luther King, Jr. Create a dialogue between the two men that illustrates their differing beliefs on how to gain freedom for African American people.

Cross-curricular Connections

Math: Mecca, which is the holy land for Muslims is 7,145 miles from Atlanta, GA. If you were in a plane traveling 400 miles an hour. How many hours would it take you to get to Mecca from Atlanta?

Science: Malcolm X had reddish hair. Research what causes people to have different hair colors.

Stokley Carmichael/Kwame Ture

If you have ever heard anyone use the term "Black Power" then you are experiencing only a fraction of the impact that Stokley Carmichael has had on American society. Carmichael spent a relatively short time in the United States fighting for the freedom of African Americans but his impact and influence is undeniable. Stokley's charismatic personality, militant beliefs, and uncompromising dedication to the freedom of black people everywhere forced the nation to deal with its treatment of its African American citizens in a way that it never had before.

Stokley Carmichael was born on June 29, 1941 in Port of Spain, the capital city on the island of Trinidad and Tobago. When he was only a toddler, both of his parents moved to New York City in search of better opportunities. They left young Stokley to be raised by his grandmother until the age of 11 when they sent for him to come live with them in New York. While in New York, he and his family lived in a mostly white neighborhood where he attended one of the most prestigious high schools in the city. Stokley excelled at academics and received several scholarships to some of the best colleges in the country, including Howard University an HBCU in Washington DC, the school he ultimately chose to attend.

While at Howard, he was quickly impressed and inspired by students participating in sit ins throughout the south and wanted to join them. As a result, while still only a freshman, Stokley joined the Freedom Riders, a group of black and white activists who rode around the south challenging the segregation policies that many bus stations still upheld, despite being ruled unconstitutional by the Supreme Court. Stokley was arrested during a ride in Mississippi and sent to jail for forty-nine days, which only reinvigorated him to continue the fight for African Americans' civil rights.

Upon his graduation from Howard University in 1964, Stokley immediately joined the Student Nonviolent Coordinating Committee (SNCC) and assisted them as they embarked on what they were calling "Freedom Summer," an aggressive campaign to register black voters in the south. Stokley became a field organizer in Lowndes County, Alabama, and impressively raised the number of registered voters from 70 to 2600 in just one year.

While Stokley was in SNCC, he worked closely with Dr. Martin Luther King, Jr., and followed his theory of nonviolent resistance. However, over time he became dissatisfied with this idea due in part to the constant humiliation, harassment, and abuse that he and his fellow activists were forced to endure at the hands of racist white men and women. Stokley began to take a more militant stance on how black people should gain their civil rights and who should be included to help obtain those rights; which is why when he was elected to be the national chairman of SNCC in 1966 he kicked out all the white members.

Stokley's major departure from Dr. King and his philosophies came while he was giving a speech in Greenwood, Mississippi after participating in James Meredith's "Walk Against Fear." In his speech he said, "We been saying 'freedom' for six years. What we are going to start saying now is 'Black Power'." The term "Black Power" became Stokley's rallying cry to motivate and energize the younger, more radical activists in the Civil Rights Movement. He said that Black Power was "a call for black people in this country to unite, to recognize their heritage, to build a sense of community. It is a call for black people to define their own goals, and lead their own organizations." Stokley calling for Black Power also broke from Dr. King's ideas about integration and nonviolence, shifting the movement toward one of self-defense and separation, two philosophies that had been advocated by Malcolm X. This caused a major rift in the Civil Rights Movement between the younger activists who sided with Carmichael and the older ones who sided with Dr. King.

In 1967 Carmichael traveled to Cuba, Vietnam, China and Guinea to meet with the leaders of those countries and to discuss with them their ideas on revolution. Those conversations helped shape

Carmichael's plans for what he believed was necessary for black people in the United States to gain their freedom. When he came back to the United States, he left SNCC and became the Prime Minister of the Black Panther Party. In his role as Prime Minister he toured the country giving speeches about black nationalism, black separatism and Pan Africanism, the belief that all people of African descent should unite against their common oppressor and work to uplift black people everywhere.

In 1969, Stokley Carmichael left the Black Panther Party and the United States and moved to Conakry, Guinea in West Africa. He changed his name to Kwame Ture in honor of the Ghanaian president, Kwame Nkrumah and Guinea president, Sekou Toure. From this point on Kwame Ture dedicated his life to fostering African unity across the globe, a fight he waged until his death from prostate cancer in 1998.

Kwame Ture was an electric orator, prolific writer, uncompromising activist and a master organizer. He showed the country that there was more than one path to freedom and that his path required courage, relentless perseverance, and above all else: Black Power.

Show What You Know! – Stokley Carmichael/Kwame Ture

Reading for Understanding

1. What caused Stokley Carmichael to join the Civil Rights Movement?

   _____
   _____
   _____

2. Who were the Freedom Riders and what was their main goal?

   _____
   _____
   _____

3. What was Freedom Summer?

   _____
   _____
   _____

4. Do you think Stokley's push for Black Power was a good idea? Explain your answer.

   _____
   _____
   _____

5. How was Stokley's philosophy about Civil Rights different at the end of his life compared to when he first joined the movement?

   _____
   _____
   _____

Take it to the Next Level

1. Make a Black Power poster. On your poster include a symbol, and three statements that are related to the Black Power movement.
2. Create a fictional social media account for Stokley Carmichael. Include a picture, things he would like and dislike, friends he might have, activities he would be involved in, personal information, etc.
3. What does Black Power mean to you? Write a paragraph explaining what your philosophy on Black Power and how it can be used to improve the situation in the black community.

Cross-curricular Connections

Math: Stokley Carmichael helped to raise the voting population in Lowndes County Alabama from 70 to 2600 in a single year. What percent increase is that?

Science: Stokley Carmichael died from complications due to prostate cancer. What causes prostate cancer? How can someone prevent themselves from getting prostate cancer? What are the symptoms of someone who has it? How can it be treated once someone gets prostate cancer?

Fannie Lou Hamer

One could not have a conversation about the impact and contributions of women on the Civil Rights Movement and not mention Fannie Lou Hamer. Her fiery spirit, unrelenting determination, and fearlessness in the face of extreme racism and violence earned her a place right next to other activists of her time such as Martin Luther King, Jr. and Stokley Carmichael.

The youngest of 20 children, Fannie Lou Townsend was born on October 6, 1917 in Montgomery County, Mississippi. Both of her parents, like many other African Americans in the deep south at that time, were sharecroppers. They were allowed to farm and live on the land owned by a white person in exchange for giving the owner a portion of the crop at the end of each year. They were not usually paid, and any supplies, tools, or additional food that they required had to be obtained from the land owner on credit, which usually plunged black families deeper and deeper into debt. Fannie Lou was very familiar with this system as she started working in the fields at the young age of six, and even dropped out of school at the age of twelve to work full time in the field to help her family.

In 1944, she married Perry Hamer and became Fannie Lou Hamer. They continued to work as sharecroppers picking cotton in the Mississippi Delta. Fannie Lou Hamer desperately wanted to start a family but couldn't have children of her own due to having her uterus removed against her will and without her consent when she went to the hospital to have surgery to have a tumor extracted. This horrible and illegal procedure was done to hundreds of black women by racist doctors who thought they were doing the world a favor by not allowing black women to have any more children.

During the summer of 1962, Fannie Lou attended a meeting hosted by the Student Nonviolent Coordinating Committee (SNCC) who were encouraging black people in the south to register to vote. It was at this meeting that she found out that black people were actually guaranteed the right to vote according to the 15th Amendment to the Constitution of the United States; information that had been purposefully kept from her by the white land owners she had been working for. Inspired by this meeting, she and seventeen others promptly went down to the county courthouse and tried to become registered. Despite the intimidation tactics used by the courthouse clerks, Fannie Lou registered to vote. Once the white people in town found out what she had done, they immediately got her fired from her job and kicked her off the plantation that she had called home for the last twenty years.

Undeterred, Fannie Lou became even more motivated to become involved in the Civil Rights Movement. She stated, "They kicked me off the plantation, they set me free. It's the best thing that could happen. Now I can work for my people." She began working for SNCC as an organizer where she spearheaded voter registration drives and relief efforts. During her time with SNCC she was arrested, threatened, beaten, and shot at. On one occasion when she was returning from a voter registration workshop in South Carolina, she and her colleagues refused to move out of the whites only section of the bus station. When they were arrested and taken to jail, the white police officers made two black prisoners beat Fannie Lou and the other activists mercilessly with clubs. Fannie Lou nearly died and never fully recovered from the incident, losing vision in one of her eyes, and suffering permanent kidney damage.

Fannie Lou believed that voting and political representation was essential for African Americans to improve their status throughout the south. In 1963, Fannie Lou helped found the Mississippi Freedom Democratic Party, which was to serve as an alternative to Mississippi's all white delegation that they were sending to the Democratic National Convention. In conjunction with her party's arrival at the convention, she also announced that she was running for congress. She used her platform to make the convention and other candidates address the issues of racism and discrimination that were plaguing Mississippi. During the convention she gave an impassioned televised speech that addressed the issues of voter suppression and state sanctioned violence against African Americans. The speech was intentionally interrupted with the hope of silencing her message by President Lyndon Johnson, claiming that he wanted to give an impromptu press conference. To the president's dismay, the entire speech was later replayed on the evening news.

With barely a grade school education, Fannie Lou Hamer proved that a person's worth is not determined by how many degrees they have, but rather how they stand up in the face of adversity and injustice. Driven by her famous phrase, "I'm sick and tired of being sick and tired," Ms. Hamer was a mighty force in the Civil Rights Movement and was unrelenting in her fight for justice and equality for African Americans.

Show What You Know! – Fannie Lou Hamer

Reading for Understanding

1. Describe the system of sharecropping.

    _____

    _____

    _____

2. Why couldn't Mrs. Hamer have children?

    _____

    _____

    _____

3. What did the 15th Amendment do?

    _____

    _____

    _____

4. What prompted Mrs. Hamer to get involved in the Civil Rights Movement?

    _____

    _____

    _____

5. What was the purpose of forming the Mississippi Freedom Democratic Party?

    _____

    _____

    _____

Take it to the Next Level

1. Listen to the speech Mrs. Hamer made at the Democratic National Convention and write a paragraph describing your reaction to what she said.
2. Create a children's book describing the life of Fannie Lou Hamer.
3. Mrs. Hamer's most famous phrase is "I'm sick and tired of being sick and tired." Research three more sayings or quotes from here and explain what they mean to you.

Cross-curricular Connections

Math: In 1962, only 6.7% of the eligible black voters in Mississippi were registered to vote. If the black population in Mississippi at that time was 915,000, how many black people could vote at in 1962?
Science: Black women throughout history have been mistreated by doctors like the one who operated on Mrs. Hamer. Research other incidents where black women have been experimented on and abused by members of the medical profession because of their racist views.

The Black Panther Party

As far as civil rights groups go, the Black Panther Party for Self-Defense is often one of the most misunderstood groups of that era. Founded in 1966 in Oakland, California by Merritt Junior College students Huey P. Newton and Bobby Seale, the Black Panthers' original goal was to protect black people in their community from police harassment and violence.

Like other areas of the country in the 1960s, black people in Oakland, California were suffering from racism, joblessness, social inequality, and police brutality. In the wake of the Watts Riots, sparked by police having a violent encounter with a black motorist and his pregnant mother, black people in the urban centers of California were especially sensitive to the racist actions of police officers. As a response, Huey Newton and Bobby Seale instructed members of their newly formed Black Panther Party for Self-Defense to patrol their communities, follow police officers known for their racist practices, and protect those black citizens who were being abused by law enforcement.

Often seen in their unofficial uniform of black leather jackets, black berets, and black sunglasses, the Black Panthers evoked feelings of intimidation and fear from many white Americans. However, contrary to popular belief, the Black Panther Party was not a violent organization. While they did believe in carrying firearms, a right guaranteed to all citizens by the Second Amendment to the Constitution, they did not believe in being violent toward anyone who was not violent toward them. Following the teaching of Malcolm X, they believed in self-defense and defending their community against people that would do it harm. It is from this idea that they chose the symbol of the panther, a jungle cat that does not strike unless it is provoked.

Soon Newton and Seale began to focus their attention on more than just police brutality. Influenced by the teachings of Karl Marx, the two men believed that the main problem facing black people was economic exploitation and that if they could dismantle capitalism that black people would be on a level playing field with everyone else. It was this philosophy, combined with a sense of social justice that led to the creation of the Black Panther Party's 10 Point Plan:

1. **We want freedom. We want power to determine the destiny of our black community.**
2. **We want full employment for our people.**
3. **We want an end to the robbery by the capitalists of our black community.**
4. **We want decent housing fit for the shelter of human beings.**
5. **We want education for our people that exposes the true nature of this decadent American society. We want education that teaches us our true history and our role in present day society.**
6. **We want all black men to be exempt from military service.**
7. **We want an immediate end to police brutality and murder of black people.**
8. **We want freedom for all black men held in federal, state, county, and city prisons and jails.**
9. **We want all black people when brought to trial to be tried in a court by a jury of their peer group or people from their black communities, as defined by the constitution of the United States.**
10. **We want land, bread, housing, education, clothing, justice, and peace.**

The Panthers established several programs designed to solve many of the problems affecting the black community. They created a newspaper entitled *The Black Panther*, a free health care clinic, a free ambulance service, free legal service, a shoe program, transportation assistance, education programs, and a free breakfast program for school children that was so popular that it spread to several cities across the country.

As the Black Panthers began to gain national popularity, they also grabbed the attention of the Director of the FBI, J. Edgar Hoover. He had the Panthers labeled as an enemy of the state due to their beliefs in certain communist ideas. He also said that "the Black Panther Party without question represents the greatest threat to the internal security of the country." Through his domestic counterintelligence agency, COINTELPRO, Hoover set out to disrupt and dismantle the Black Panther Party by infiltrating it with spies and double agents.

In the late 1960s the FBI and police stepped up their already aggressive methods, and many Panther members were jailed, beaten, or killed. On a cold early morning in December of 1969, Chicago Panther Party leaders Mark Clark and Fred Hampton were killed in a raid by police that lasted almost 5 hours. During the raid, 82-99 bullets were fired by the police and only 1 shot came from inside the house. This event symbolized the end of the Black Panther Party. While remnants of the group still exist today, it no longer has the same impact and influence as it once did.

Show What You Know! – The Black Panther Party

Reading for Understanding

1. Who started the Black Panther Party and what was its original purpose?
   _____
   _____
   _____

2. What was the Black Panther's stance on using violence?
   _____
   _____
   _____

3. Which of their 10 points do you think is the most important and why?
   _____
   _____
   _____

4. What programs did the Panthers establish to help the community?
   _____
   _____
   _____

5. How was COINTELPRO used against the Black Panthers?
   _____
   _____
   _____

Take it to the Next Level

1. Create your own 10-point plan of what you think is needed in order to improve things in your community?
2. The Black Panthers were created to stop police violence in their community. What do you think can be done to stop the police violence and brutality that is occurring in black communities across the country? Write a paragraph explaining your answer.
3. Write a rap or poem that describes the Panther's 10 Point Plan.

Cross-curricular Connections

Math: At its height, the Black Panther Party's free breakfast program provided 10,000 students breakfast in a single day. If there are approximately 180 school days in a year, how many breakfasts did the Panthers serve in one year?

Science: Research the benefits of a child receiving breakfast before going to school on their educational success.

Printed in the USA
CPSIA information can be obtained
at www.ICGtesting.com
JSHW060512240823
47067JS00004B/34